10/02

THE
PIMA-MARICOPA

THE PIMA-MARICOPA

Henry F. Dobyns
D'Arcy McNickle Center for the
History of the American Indian
The Newberry Library

Frank W. Porter III
General Editor

CHELSEA HOUSE PUBLISHERS
New York   Philadelphia

On the cover A maze basket and a beaded basket
showing mounted figure

Chelsea House Publishers
Editor-in-Chief Nancy Toff
Executive Editor Remmel T. Nunn
Managing Editor Karyn Gullen Browne
Copy Chief Juliann Barbato
Picture Editor Adrian G. Allen
Art Director Maria Epes
Manufacturing Manager Gerald Levine

Indians of North America
Senior Editor Marjorie P. K. Weiser

Staff for **THE PIMA-MARICOPA**
Assistant Editor James M. Cornelius
Deputy Copy Chief Ellen Scordato
Editorial Assistant Claire M. Wilson
Designer Donna Sinisgalli
Design Assistant James Baker
Picture Researcher Margalit Fox
Production Coordinator Joseph Romano

7 9 8 6

Library of Congress Cataloging-in-Publication Data

Dobyns, Henry F.
The Pima-Maricopa / by Henry F. Dobyns.
  p. cm.—(Indians of North America)
Bibliography: p.
Includes index.
Summary: Examines the culture, history and changing
fortunes of the Pima and Maricopa Indians.
1. Pima Indians—Juvenile literature. 2. Maricopa Indians—
Juvenile literature. 3. Indians of North America—Southwest,
New—Juvenile literature. [1. Pima Indians. 2. Maricopa
Indians.] I. Title. II. Series: Indians of North America (Chelsea
House Publishers)
E99.P6D63 1989   88-30289
979'.00497—dc19   CIP
                               AC
ISBN   1-55546-724-5
      0-7910-0394-9 (pbk.)

CONTENTS

INDIANS OF NORTH AMERICA

CHELSEA HOUSE PUBLISHERS

INDIANS OF NORTH AMERICA: CONFLICT AND SURVIVAL

Frank W. Porter III

The Indians survived our open intention of wiping them out, and since the tide turned they have even weathered our good intentions toward them, which can be much more deadly.

John Steinbeck
America and Americans

When Europeans first reached the North American continent, they found hundreds of tribes occupying a vast and rich country. The newcomers quickly recognized the wealth of natural resources. They were not, however, so quick or willing to recognize the spiritual, cultural, and intellectual riches of the people they called Indians.

The Indians of North America examines the problems that develop when people with different cultures come together. For American Indians, the consequences of their interaction with non-Indian people have been both productive and tragic. The Europeans believed they had "discovered" a "New World," but their religious bigotry, cultural bias, and materialistic world view kept them from appreciating and understanding the people who lived in it. All too often they attempted to change the way of life of the indigenous people. The Spanish conquistadores wanted the Indians as a source of labor. The Christian missionaries, many of whom were English, viewed them as potential converts. French traders and trappers used the Indians as a means to obtain pelts. As Francis Parkman, the 19th-century historian, stated, "Spanish civilization crushed the Indian; English civilization scorned and neglected him; French civilization embraced and cherished him."

7

Nearly 500 years later, many people think of American Indians as curious vestiges of a distant past, waging a futile war to survive in a Space Age society. Even today, our understanding of the history and culture of American Indians is too often derived from unsympathetic, culturally biased, and inaccurate reports. The American Indian, described and portrayed in thousands of movies, television programs, books, articles, and government studies, has either been raised to the status of the "noble savage" or disparaged as the "wild Indian" who resisted the westward expansion of the American frontier.

Where in this popular view are the real Indians, the human beings and communities whose ancestors can be traced back to ice-age hunters? Where are the creative and indomitable people whose sophisticated technologies used the natural resources to ensure their survival, whose military skill might even have prevented European settlement of North America if not for devastating epidemics and disruption of the ecology? Where are the men and women who are today diligently struggling to assert their legal rights and express once again the value of their heritage?

The various Indian tribes of North America, like people everywhere, have a history that includes population expansion, adaptation to a range of regional environments, trade across wide networks, internal strife, and warfare. This was the reality. Europeans justified their conquests, however, by creating a mythical image of the New World and its native people. In this myth, the New World was a virgin land, waiting for the Europeans. The arrival of Christopher Columbus ended a timeless primitiveness for the original inhabitants.

Also part of this myth was the debate over the origins of the American Indians. Fantastic and diverse answers were proposed by the early explorers, missionairies, and settlers. Some thought that the Indians were descended from the Ten Lost Tribes of Israel, others that they were descended from inhabitants of the lost continent of Atlantis. One writer suggested that the Indians had reached North America in another Noah's ark.

A later myth, perpetrated by many historians, focused on the relentless persecution during the past five centuries until only a scattering of these "primitive" people remained to be herded onto reservations. This view fails to chronicle the overt and covert ways in which the Indians successfully coped with the intruders.

All of these myths presented one-sided interpretations that ignored the complexity of European and American events and policies. All left serious questions unanswered. What were the origins of the American Indians? Where did they come from? How and when did they get to the New World? What was their life—their culture—really like?

In the late 1800s, anthropologists and archaeologists in the Smithsonian Institution's newly created Bureau of American Ethnology in Washington,

D.C., began to study scientifically the history and culture of the Indians of North America. They were motivated by an honest belief that the Indians were on the verge of extinction and that along with them would vanish their languages, religious beliefs, technology, myths, and legends. These men and women went out to visit, study, and record data from as many Indian communities as possible before this information was forever lost.

By this time there was a new myth in the national consciousness. American Indians existed as figures in the American past. They had performed a historical mission. They had challenged white settlers who trekked across the continent. Once conquered, however, they were supposed to accept graciously the way of life of their conquerors.

The reality again was different. American Indians resisted both actively and passively. They refused to lose their unique identity, to be assimilated into white society. Many whites viewed the Indians not only as members of a conquered nation but also as "inferior" and "unequal." The rights of the Indians could be expanded, contracted, or modified as the conquerors saw fit. In every generation, white society asked itself what to do with the American Indians. Their answers have resulted in the twists and turns of federal Indian policy.

There were two general approaches. One way was to raise the Indians to a "higher level" by "civilizing" them. Zealous missionaries considered it their Christian duty to elevate the Indian through conversion and scanty education. The other approach was to ignore the Indians until they disappeared under pressure from the ever-expanding white society. The myth of the "vanishing Indian" gave stronger support to the latter option, helping to justify the taking of the Indians' land.

Prior to the end of the 18th century, there was no national policy on Indians simply because the American nation has not yet come into existence. American Indians similarly did not possess a political or social unity with which to confront the various Europeans. They were not homogeneous. Rather, they were loosely formed bands and tribes, speaking nearly 300 languages and thousands of dialects. The collective identity felt by Indians today is a result of their common experiences of defeat and/or mistreatment at the hands of whites.

During the colonial period, the British crown did not have a coordinated policy toward the Indians of North America. Specific tribes (most notably the Iroquois and the Cherokee) became military and political pawns used by both the crown and the individual colonies. The success of the American Revolution brought no immediate change. When the United States acquired new territory from France and Mexico in the early 19th century, the federal government wanted to open this land to settlement by homesteaders. But the Indian tribes that lived on this land had signed treaties with European governments assuring their title to the land. Now the United States assumed legal responsibility for honoring these treaties.

At first, President Thomas Jefferson believed that the Louisiana Purchase contained sufficient land for both the Indians and the white population. Within a generation, though, it became clear that the Indians would not be allowed to remain. In the 1830s the federal government began to coerce the eastern tribes to sign treaties agreeing to relinquish their ancestral land and move west of the Mississippi River. Whenever these negotiations failed, President Andrew Jackson used the military to remove the Indians. The southeastern tribes, promised food and transportation during their removal to the West, were instead forced to walk the "Trail of Tears." More than 4,000 men, woman, and children died during this forced march. The "removal policy" was successful in opening the land to homesteaders, but it created enormous hardships for the Indians.

By 1871 most of the tribes in the United States had signed treaties ceding most or all of their ancestral land in exchange for reservations and welfare. The treaty terms were intended to bind both parties for all time. But in the General Allotment Act of 1887, the federal government changed its policy again. Now the goal was to make tribal members into individual landowners and farmers, encouraging their absorption into white society. This policy was advantageous to whites who were eager to acquire Indian land, but it proved disastrous for the Indians. One hundred thirty-eight million acres of reservation land were subdivided into tracts of 160, 80, or as little as 40 acres, and allotted tribe members on an individual basis. Land owned in this way was said to have "trust status" and could not be sold. But the surplus land—all Indian land not allotted to individuals—was opened (for sale) to white settlers. Ultimately, more than 90 million acres of land were taken from the Indians by legal and illegal means.

The resulting loss of land was a catastrophe for the Indians. It was necessary to make it illegal for Indians to sell their land to non-Indians. The Indian Reorganization Act of 1934 officially ended the allotment period. Tribes that voted to accept the provisions of this act were reorganized, and an effort was made to purchase land within preexisting reservations to restore an adequate land base.

Ten years later, in 1944, federal Indian policy again shifted. Now the federal government wanted to get out of the "Indian business." In 1953 an act of Congress named specific tribes whose trust status was to be ended "at the earliest possible time." This new law enabled the United States to end unilaterally, whether the Indians wished it or not, the special status that protected the land in Indian tribal reservations. In the 1950s federal Indian policy was to transfer federal responsibility and jurisdiction to state governments, encourage the physical relocation of Indian peoples from reservations to urban areas, and hasten the termination, or extinction, of tribes.

Between 1954 and 1962 Congress passed specific laws authorizing the termination of more than 100 tribal groups. The stated purpose of the termination policy was to ensure the full and complete integration of Indians into American society. However, there is a less benign way to interpret this legislation. Even as termination was being discussed in Congress, 133 separate bills were introduced to permit the transfer of trust land ownership from Indians to non-Indians.

With the Johnson administration in the 1960s the federal government began to reject termination. In the 1970s yet another Indian policy emerged. Known as "self-determination," it favored keeping the protective role of the federal government while increasing tribal participation in, and control of, important areas of local government. In 1983 President Reagan, in a policy statement on Indian affairs, restated the unique "government is government" relationship of the United States with the Indians. However, federal programs since then have moved toward transferring Indian affairs to individual states, which have long desired to gain control of Indian land and resources.

As long as American Indians retain power, land, and resources that are coveted by the states and the federal government, there will continue to be a "clash of cultures," and the issues will be contested in the courts, Congress, the White House, and even in the international human rights community. To give all Americans a greater comprehension of the issues and conflicts involving American Indians today is a major goal of this series. These issues are not easily understood, nor can these conflicts be readily resolved. The study of North American Indian history and culture is a necessary and important step toward that comprehension. All Americans must learn the history of the relations between the Indians and the federal government, recognize the unique legal status of the Indians, and understand the heritage and cultures of the Indians of North America.

El Picacho (Spanish, "the Peak"), on the edge of the Sonoran desert in what is now southern Arizona, is a landmark of Pima and Maricopa territory.

1

FEEDING FORTY-NINERS

Forty-niners following the Southern Wagon Road across what was then northwestern Mexico to the California goldfields became frantic after they passed the Picacho. This peak rises starkly above the desert plain 40 miles north of Tucson, then a Mexican frontier military post. The alien environment, so hot and dry, caused great anxiety to the tired travelers, but fear of attack by hostile Indians was far more unsettling. Companies formed for mutual defense by friends and neighbors who had traveled together for hundreds of miles began to disperse into small squads, moving without any order. With no grass or water, the migrants' draft animals broke down. Those who had wagons harnessed their spare animals and abandoned the exhausted livestock.

The working animals had last drunk nine miles north of Tucson at Point of Mountain water hole, where the surface flow of the Santa Cruz River vanished into the sand. Wise travelers left there around sunset and kept going all night and the next day, "to have the advantage of the coolness of the night and shade," in the words of one member of Isaac Duval's Texas company. Duval's group traveled for some 24 hours, covering 70 miles before resting the second night.

The migrants' greater fear was first tested before they reached the Gila River at 10:00 the following morning. Indians were approaching.

Many forty-niners carried copies of the report written by Lieutenant William H. Emory, who had been the official journalist for Brigadier General Stephen W. Kearny's Army of the West. Kearny's troops had traveled this route three years earlier, descending the Gila River from New Mexico en route to the Pacific Coast, where they fought against Mexicans on behalf of the United States. Perhaps 20,000 of the adventurers who set off for California after gold was discovered near Sacramento took the southern route, across

The Pima used gourds as water and storage vessels. The fruit of a plant found in the Sonoran desert, gourds make ideal containers when dried and hollowed out.

northwestern Mexico. Emory had described the Indians his troops met, so when Duval's group saw Indians approaching, they hurriedly reread Emory's 1846 descriptions of the Apache,

Pima, and Maricopa. Every forty-niner feared a meeting with the Apache, who raided migrant caravans and camps for horses, mules, weapons, and supplies. The Pima and Maricopa, two allied tribes, were known to be friendly.

The travelers' alarm changed to relief when they saw that the approaching Indians carried gourds, pumpkins, and corn—not weapons. Here, surely, were the friendly Pima described in Emory's report.

"*Amigos. Amigos.*" The Pima shouted the Spanish word for "friends." The forty-niners, some of whom spoke Spanish or had learned this word at Tucson or somewhere farther east, responded:

"Amigos."

Members of Duval's company gratefully drank water from the gourds that served the Pima as canteens. They relished the sweet, moist, roasted pumpkin and green corn. After serving refreshing food and drink, the Pima left the group of Texans, hurrying farther along the wagon ruts to seek out other travelers in need of help. As they went, the Pima found and fed abandoned horses, mules, and oxen, then led them to the Gila River for water.

On Sunday morning, July 15, another party of weary migrants, having traveled 65 miles from Tucson, was uncertain how far they had to go to reach the Gila. Indians appeared. Again, the travelers consulted Emory's report and smiled with relief. Mercy riders holding watermelons must be Pima!

These travelers, in real distress until their meeting with the Pima, feasted on cool, watery melons, then fed the rinds to their hungry stock. Their mood shifted from pessimism to optimism; men and beasts felt refreshed.

The forty-niners could not understand most of the words spoken by the Pima mercy patrol, but the Indians' encouraging gestures conveyed their meaning: "Follow the wagon ruts straight ahead to the river." Travelers bound for California goldfields did just that. Later, a number of them would write accounts of the difficult trek through the desert, praising the Pima who greeted and supported them.

There was not much grass near the river, one noted, "but the Indians fetched us plenty of corn fodder for our animals." Pima men, women, and children crowded into the migrants' camps offering to trade melons and baskets filled with maize or beans for beads, cloth, blankets, or shirts. The travelers eagerly feasted on roasting ears (corn) and other food.

Confident of the Pima's friendliness, the groups scattered through the area. Some advanced a few miles and camped close to the nearest Pima village. Most stopped by the stream to rest their livestock. Those who had abandoned weakened animals that the Pima

A Pima village in 1864. The women each carry a kihau, *or burden basket. At right is the* ramada, *a shade for animals that also served as a workplace for people.*

had not retrieved now returned to the desert in the hope of finding their valuable beasts and leading them to the oasis.

These forty-niners took their time traveling through the Gila River oasis that was home to the Indians of the Pima-Maricopa Confederation. For 4 days they rested, fed their animals maize stalks for which they paid 25 cents per bundle, traded for a wide variety of provisions, and moved only as far as 20 miles west to the last Maricopa village. They were then ready to embark on the trail west to California.

Even those forty-niners who had read Emory's report were, as one of them wrote, "all very agreeably surprised to see such an extensive settlement of what is called the wild Indian, surpassing many of the Christian nations in agriculture and little behind them in many useful arts." The Pima farmers they saw were industrious, as their well-supplied villages demonstrated.

The forty-niners may not have realized it, but the Pima and Maricopa had already acquired such staples of Old World agriculture as livestock and wheat and had adapted these to their traditional farming procedures. The Indians made good use of the rivers near their oasis, drawing the waters off into ditches to irrigate their fields. They raised horses, mules, and cattle. They yoked oxen to simple wooden plows to cultivate the soil. They made wooden harrows to break up the plowed earth

and weeded their crops with straight-handled hoes. By mid-July 1849 the Pima had acquired a stock of steel axes and iron shovels by trading with forty-niners and had quickly learned to make good use of these more efficient farming tools.

Curious travelers visited Pima households and described what they saw: "Each abode consists of a dome shaped wicker-work about six feet high and from 20 to 50 feet in diameter, thatched with straw or cornstalks." Inside these houses were "large earthen-ware jars &c, baskets filled with mesquite beans, corn, wheat, and some fine melons," plentiful food supplies being stored for later use.

Near most houses stood "a large arbor open on all sides." The arbor roofs served as drying platforms on which the Pima piled maize, cotton in the boll, and wheat straw. Women did most of their household chores in the shade of such arbors when they were not away from the village, working in fields near the river or harvesting giant cactus fruits on desert hillsides.

One forty-niner was "much amused" to watch "an old granny" who sat "down on her legs" to make a special treat. She dipped wheat from an earthen pot in which it had been boiled, then placed the grains on a milling stone. She rolled a small, smooth stone over the grains to mash them, "dipping her hand occasionally in a vessel of the thin watery kind of molasses." This "molasses" was a sweet syrup made from the juice of the fruit of the giant saguaro cactus. First the woman had poured the juice through a basket strainer to remove the tiny black seeds. Then she boiled it until it became thick. Using her stone much like a rolling pin, the granny formed the syrup-sweetened wheat into "rolls like stick candy or smaller."

The "little copper coloured and naked urchins all a-lying around her watching" popped the rolls into their mouths as fast as the granny made them. Although the gold-seeking migrants noticed that the Pima wore very little clothing during the heat of the Sonoran desert summer, they did not realize that their own heavy clothing increased their chances of dehydration and heat exhaustion.

The forty-niners observed many details of life in the Pima villages, but they failed to report on the Pima New Year ritual. This was probably because not one of them was invited, though it took place while they were in the area. The ceremony, held in early July, centered on a mildly alcoholic beverage made from the syrup of the saguaro fruit. Before making the syrup, the women had to carry pots to groves of the giant cactus on the southern slopes of the desert mountains. Here, guarded by armed men, the women would remain for one to three weeks.

The women lashed together two ribs of the woody "skeletons" of dead giant cacti and attached a shorter piece of rib to serve as a crossbar. Using this pole,

Harvesting Cactus Fruit—Maricopa, *a photograph by Edward Curtis, about 1907. The fruit of the saguaro cactus was a staple of their diet, and its juice was fermented to yield* navait, *a drink used in the New Year ritual.*

they pulled the ripe, fig-sized fruit from the tall plants. They then collected the fallen fruit in baskets and carried it to pots set on stones over a cooking fire. Here the women split open the bright red fruit, holding it over a basketry sieve placed on top of the pot. With their thumbs they scooped out the crimson pulp, letting it fall into the sieve. The sweet juice drained into the pot, and the sieve caught the oily, black seeds. As the juice in the pots boiled down to a sugary syrup, the women molded the cactus seeds into large cakes and put them aside to dry in the sun. Everyone feasted on the fresh cactus fruit while waiting for the syrup to thicken.

When the syrup was finished, the women poured it into storage pots and placed a large piece of broken pottery

The kihau, *or burden basket, consisted of a basketwork platform woven between framing sticks. Its unusual design allowed for carrying odd-shaped, fragile, or heavy objects.*

over the top. They sealed this lid with claylike mud or with gum from the creosote bush. Each woman carefully stacked her syrup pots in the *kihau* (burden basket) she carried on her back. The women then returned home. After all the syrup from the new crop had reached the oasis villages, the Pima could begin to plan their New Year's festival.

Village elders set the date four days in advance. During the first two days of preparation, householders carried their syrup pots to the largest structure in the village. This building was the *vahki*, which served as both a community meetinghouse and a house of worship. Inside the vahki, a brewmaster-priest poured syrup from the small pots into the very large pots that were used only once a year and only for making the beverage. He thinned the syrup with clear river water and placed the pots in holes dug into the earth floor around a fireplace. A small, steady fire was sufficient to turn the fruit sugars into alcohol within two days. While the beverage was brewing, the brewmaster-priest sang old and newly composed sacred songs.

Toward the end of the second day, the village men assembled on the dance ground in front of the vahki. They sat in four groups to form a broken circle, each group facing toward one of the four sacred directions. When the beverage, known as *navait*, was ready, the brewmaster-priest made a devout speech, asking all the men who would drink to pray for rain by becoming beautifully intoxicated. This, the Pima believed, brought winds and the rain clouds they blew across the sky. The brewmaster-priest selected special navait servers, preferably two, to serve each of the four groups of seated men.' These eight servers dipped the navait from large watertight baskets into a pottery or gourd cup for each man. As they served the liquor, they said to each man, "Drink, friend! Get beautifully drunk. Bring hither the wind and the clouds."

While the navait was being served and drunk, the men sang hymns of prayer for rain. Stimulated by the beverage, many would extemporaneously compose new drinking and prayer songs. Then they scattered to visit the homes of their friends, where they continued drinking the navait that had been prepared in each household. Women did not participate in the navait drinking ceremony, nor did they drink at home. They stayed sober, helping to maintain order in the community.

Men drank a good deal in order to become bloated with navait and then vomit the beverage. People were not appalled; instead, they approved, saying that a vomiting man had thrown up "clouds." Moistening the earth with navait in this way, they believed, would bring rain clouds to the watershed of the Gila River. The Pima perceived the arrival of rain to be a result of the return of holy liquid to earth.

In fact, the summer monsoon in the Sonoran desert usually begins in mid-July, and this served every year to confirm the validity of the Pima's belief in the effectiveness of their rain-bringing efforts. So important was the navait ritual to the Pima that they made it the beginning of their year. The Giant Cactus Fruit Harvest Moon was the first month of their 12-month year. The navait New Year celebration appears to have originated in the very distant past, suggesting that the ancient Pima had learned to depend on the fruit of the saguaro cactus well before they learned to grow domesticated plants.

The July monsoons brought an abundance of thunderstorms over the Gila River basin. The river rose enough to flow through the Pima's irrigation canals, enabling them to plow their fields and plant a second crop. Continued runoff from the river nourished the plants. As a result, the Pima usually had an ample supply of food to trade with Mexicans and with other Indian villages, as well as to offer the forty-niners passing through.

When they were not encamped in desert cactus groves, Pima and Maricopa women spent their days harvesting and preparing ripe saguaro fruits or the nutritious flower buds of the opuntia cactus in season. When they were at home in their villages near the river, they spent much of the day grinding fresh foods. Soon after they had gathered the abundant pod crop from the Gila River mesquite forest, they ground the very sweet and nutritious pith (the spongy part of the mesquite seedpod) to make flour or meal. The women mixed the meal with water and then

A Pima irrigation canal near the Gila River. For centuries the Pima and Maricopa used an extensive system of canals to bring river water to their crops.

formed it into cakes to bake. Because insects that fed on raw pods did not attack it, mesquite bread kept indefinitely. It was a staple Pima food, but few migrants liked its taste.

Women ground maize kernels into cornmeal. It could be added to soups and stews to thicken them and was used in other ways as well—cornmeal mixed with water made a refreshing drink. Women also ground wheat grains into flour to make the thin wafers called *tortillas*. They mixed the wheat flour with water and fat, patting it out on a flat stone and tossing it with both hands until it was stretched thin. Then they baked each tortilla quickly on a hot clay pan. The women traded the meal or flour they ground, whereas the men traded whole grains. The Pima women who sold or traded provisions to forty-

niners and later visitors profited from their labor at grinding.

Both Pima men and women wove cotton fiber into cloth for sheets and clothing. When they had time, they picked seeds out of the fiber pulled from stored bolls. Seated, the women embedded a mass of fibers in the sand, holding the mass under a foot. With their hands they drew a thin strand of cotton out and onto a spindle held between two toes. Twisting the spindle, they spun out a cotton thread that was impressively fine.

The Pima used the thread to weave cloth. They had two kinds of looms. Women wove cloth on a ground loom. Four stakes driven into the earth became its corner supports. Two cane beams, each about six feet long, were tied to the stakes to define the ends of the fabric. A length of thread was wrapped around the loom's beams to form the warp, or foundation of the cloth. Two women—or two girls who had learned the necessary skills—knelt at each side of the loom. A stick, or heddle, separated the alternate warp threads to form an opening. The weavers threw a two-foot-long wooden device called a shuttle back and forth through this opening. A length of cotton thread wrapped around the shuttle was the weaving thread, or weft. After each throw of the shuttle, the weavers tapped the weft tightly into place against the previously woven rows. Then they positioned the warp so the next throw of the shuttle would pull the cotton weft thread across warp threads that had not been covered the previous time.

Older men wove on a smaller belt loom. One end of the warp was wrapped over a small rod and the other end tied to a convenient post or ground peg. The weaver attached the rod securely to a belt tied around his waist. Narrow strips of cloth were produced

Pima women usually wove on a large ground loom, shown here; men used smaller belt looms. On both types of loom the Pima wove cotton and wool cloth for blankets and clothing.

in this fashion, and because the loom was so narrow the weaver handled the shuttle and changed the warp position by himself.

The Pima planted cotton soon after the mesquite trees leafed out, usually in early March, a sign that the danger of frost had passed. It took all summer for cotton plants to grow, bloom, and set (produce) bolls, so that the cotton fiber could mature. They also planted maize, beans, and pumpkins when the mesquite trees leafed out, harvesting these food crops in early summer and planting a second crop in July for harvest in the fall. Forty-niners who ate roasting ears and melons in mid-July were eating the harvest from the spring

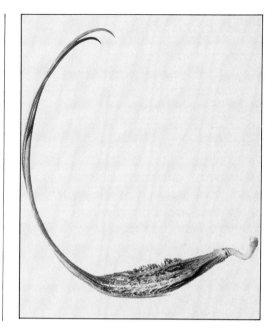

Above: *A seedpod of the* Martynia, *or devil's-claw plant, which grows wild in the Sonoran desert. The black fibers of the pod are used for making baskets. The seeds are edible.* Below: *A bundle of the pods as a craftsperson might buy it today.*

crop. Because of their different harvest times, the Pima planted cotton and food crops in different fields. They also planted melons and pumpkins in separate fields to prevent cross-pollination by bees. Cross-pollination, such as the deposit of pumpkin pollen on a melon blossom, produces inedible fruit. The Pima learned this soon after they acquired melon seeds.

Pima women also cultivated the devil's-claw plant, using the black fibers stripped from its seedpods to weave designs into their baskets. Devil's-claw grows wild in the desert, its seedpods only about four inches long. For making baskets, longer strips are easier to work with because they need fewer joins. Over many years, women selected the longest devil's-claw pods they could find. By planting seeds from these pods, they successfully domesticated the plant so that it produced seedpods a foot long, yielding black fibers much easier to weave than those of the wild variety. Pima women usually planted devil's-claw separately, but they might also leave some stray plants to grow in fields alongside other crops.

Forty-niners who passed through Pima and Maricopa villages in mid-July saw men plowing fields to plant the second crop of maize, beans, pumpkins, and melons for October harvest. In November, rains raised the river level again, allowing farmers to water their fields, plow, and sow wheat. Wheat originally grew in the Old World, so the Pima had not planted it until they ob-

tained seed from Spanish colonists. By 1775, when a Spanish military post moved to Tucson, the Pima and Maricopa were the post's principal suppliers of wheat. Wheat resists frost, as plants domesticated in the New World do not, so the Indians could grow it during the winter. They pastured livestock on growing wheat in January, irrigated the fields, then harvested in May or June. Wheat was still growing when the mesquite trees leafed out in March, so the spring crops were planted in other fields.

Pima and Maricopa children learned primarily by watching and imitating their parents and other adults. Boys and girls helped their parents and thus learned how to grow and prepare the plants that yielded both foods and fibers. Children who helped to weed the different crops soon learned the paths between winter storehouses at the edge of the oasis and the huts that served as shelters and guardhouses put up at the edges of the fields. They even learned, by close observation, to identify the footprints that each individual left in the dust.

Those children who learned fastest also listened attentively to warnings, oral history, and stories with a moral. Grandfathers said to grandsons who did not listen, "You did not come to listen. Go gather firewood."

Youths learned skills through practice. Boys used bows and arrows, hardwood war clubs, and, once they learned to ride on horseback, lances. Girls began practicing with grinding stones before they were strong enough to handle them.

Men who had slain enemies taught boys the ritual and religious reasons for purifying a warrior who killed. By the time a boy was about 10 years old, he could join the adults who danced around trophies of slain enemies that were displayed during the purifying rite. Women, sometimes three circles of them, danced nearest the trophies. Warriors danced in circles around the women. In the outermost circle of dancers were growing boys learning to take part in the rituals.

This way of life had its beginnings in the very distant past. More than 2,000 years ago, ancestors of the Pima lived in the Gila and Salt river valleys. Materials excavated at Many Rattlesnakes Village (often called Snaketown) near where Queen Creek flows into the Gila River have been dated to about 300 B.C. Evidence found at this site shows that the homes of the inhabitants were made of poles covered with thatch, much like those seen by the forty-niners in Pima villages. These early inhabitants of the river valleys in the desert of what is now southern Arizona are referred to as the Hohokam by archaeologists. *Hohokam* is a word in the Pima language that means something like "those who have gone before," or "ancestors."

The Hohokam successfully fashioned a way of life using the plants, animals, land, and scant water of the desert region. Over time, some Hohokam communities constructed ball courts and temple mounds like those in civilized Mexico and other parts of Middle America. Hohokam traders imported, among many other things, copper bells, polished stone palettes, and other items from Middle America; marine shells from the gulfs of California and Mexico; and turquoise from quarries in what are now northern New Mexico and central California. Hohokam farmers irrigated their crops with water carried in a system of more than 500 miles of main canals tapping into the Salt and Gila rivers upstream from the fields. They built dams of poles and brush to divert the stream into large canals veering at an angle from the river. The canals followed the contours of low terraces bordering the floodplain. The long, frost-free growing season of the Sonoran desert allowed the farmers to produce two food crops a year. Planting maize, beans, and other crops in March, Hohokam farmers watered them at two- to three-week intervals. They planted their second crop in late July after the summer monsoon rains began and irrigated it with thundershower runoff until crops ripened or until the first frost ended the growing season by killing the plants.

Descendants of Hohokam pioneers continued gardening with Gila River water diverted into a succession of canals. They continued to live in pole-and-thatch houses that changed little until the 12th century. Then the people in the area began to put up buildings of a very different kind, multistory structures with earthen walls. They carried enormous quantities of moistened, lime-impregnated mud for miles from the riverbank. They "puddled" and shaped the mud, probably between wooden forms, into layers two feet thick. Adding layers, the Hohokam were able to raise earthen structures that towered three and four stories above the floodplain.

By 1846, when Lieutenant Emory passed through the area with Kearny's Army of the West, such multistory buildings lay in ruins. Riding down the Gila River through Pima-Maricopa pasture lands on November 10, he recorded that "along the whole day's march were remains of zequias [irrigation ditches], pottery, and other evidences of a once densely populated country." Halting about noon, Emory saw "the remains of a three-story mud house, 60 feet square, pierced for doors and windows. The walls were four feet thick, and formed by layers of mud, two feet thick." The next day he visited what he called "the ruins of another Casa Montezuma."

This *Casa Grande* (big house), now Casa Grande Ruins National Monument, had been "a four-story building, as large as a castle" when Father Eusebio Francisco Kino saw it in 1694. "It is said that the ancestors of Montezuma deserted and depopulated it," Kino wrote. Montezuma, the ruler of Mexico when the Spanish arrived, had nothing

In 1701, Eusebio Francisco Kino, a Spanish Jesuit, drafted one of the earliest maps of what was then northwestern New Spain (now northern Mexico and the southwestern United States). He labeled the area at center-right Pimeria, or the land of the Pima.

to do with Casa Grande. Kino confused matters with the very first written reference to the middle Gila River valley.

That casa grande did not stand alone. Kino saw or heard of about seven or eight other such "old houses or whole cities." Actually, the Salt River valley contained more than that number. Entering the Northern Pima Christian mission field in 1687, Kino probably was not aware that the Southern Pima (distinguished from their northern kin by a different dialect) were still using such structures when Jesuits

The ruins of Casa Grande *(Big House) at Blackwater Village, as sketched in 1864. Once a four-story structure, built perhaps as early as the 12th century, it served the Indians as a fort, warehouse, and residence. It was abandoned sometime between 1625 and 1650.*

began living among them in 1624. One of these early missionaries described the dried-clay structures he saw: "Their houses are better and stronger than those of other nations, with walls of great *adobes*, which they make of clay, and roof with earth-covered terraces."

The first missionaries among the Southern Pima also described how natives stored emergency foods in the massive walled community warehouses, and they reported on the military advantage of the upper terraces. Defenders could shoot arrows through openings in the protective outer parapets, and gravity enhanced the speed of these missiles hurtling down upon assailants outside.

Apparently both Northern and Southern Pima abandoned their mas-

sive redoubts (defensive structures) some time between 1624 and 1694 and returned to building the smaller pole-and-thatch homes instead. The burned-out roofing at Casa Grande reflects the most likely reason: The Pima learned that colonial Spaniards burned houses in which someone died—a crude way of reducing the risk of contagious disease. By the 18th century, burning a deceased person's house and personal possessions had become a firmly established Pima custom. Pole-and-thatch dwellings were flammable, but thick earthen walls were not.

Spaniards and Indians both took whatever precautions they were able to against epidemic diseases. Some Southern Pima migrated south to colonial New Spain (Mexico) in 1615, probably because the epidemic of bubonic plague that began around Mexico City in 1613 had spread northward. The Pima did not comprehend that they were moving toward the disease's origin. Their intention was to reach a Christian mission where a priest might invoke supernatural protection against the affliction; both Indians and Catholics believed it was due to a divine power. Scarlet fever killed many natives in 1637, followed by widespread smallpox in 1639. The Pima probably began burning homes where a person had died some time during this period. Casa Grande at Gila River probably stood vacant by 1650.

The people of Many Rattlesnakes Village who abandoned their casa grande located their pole-and-thatch *rancheria* (settlement) near the river's north bank, away from both Casa Grande and the older village. Like earlier Hohokam, they cremated the bodies of some people who died, collecting any unburned bone and charcoal in pottery vessels and burying them. Charcoal from one such funerary urn excavated at Many Rattlesnakes Village has been dated to 1660.

The Jesuit missionaries who described how the Southern Pima used redoubt-warehouses in the 1620s also described how they cultivated *agave* plants for food. This plant is cut off at the roots and stripped of its leaves, revealing the edible core. Agave cores are roasted for up to four days in a fire pit dug into the earth and covered with leaves. Alert archaeologists have dug up evidence that the Hohokam who

built adobe casas grandes also cultivated agave in the Gila and Santa Cruz river valleys. Mountain-dwelling Southern Pima still cultivate agave, but Northern Pima stopped growing them, apparently at about the time they abandoned their earth-walled casas grandes.

Archaeologists who maintain that the middle Gila River valley's Casa Grande was abandoned in the early 1600s have not considered all available evidence. For one thing, native people elsewhere in the Americas, from Peru to Mexico, stopped building such labor-demanding structures for their rulers at this time and returned to living in simpler dwellings such as those their ancestors had inhabited. Archaeologists who take only a regional perspective do not see Hohokam developments as one of thousands of similar long-term cultural developments.

Another misinterpretation concerns fragments, or potsherds, of a particular type of Hopi ceramic that have been found at a number of "classic" Hohokam sites. (The Hopi originally lived in what is now northeastern Arizona.) Such finds are evidence of a continuing active trade of manufactured goods among the people of the Southwest. Hopi potters at Sikyatki Pueblo made distinctive and beautiful Jeddito Yellow Ware pottery types, until they began painting new floral designs known as San Bernardo Polychrome after Franciscan missionaries arrived. Ceramic analysts date the transition to 1625, but it must have taken at least a generation for floral designs to catch on. The shift was probably hastened by the death of many potters in the scarlet fever and smallpox epidemics of the 1630s.

Thus, the ceramic evidence indicates that classic Hohokam redoubt-warehouses were used until 1650. The changes in both the dwelling and pottery styles result from two likely causes: Populations were reduced by high mortality in epidemics, and colonial officials ordered the use of European styles. But, as one longtime student of Hohokam remains has observed, just because Casa Grande was abandoned does not mean that the people who had lived there disappeared. Though it has not been easy for archaeologists to connect surviving Pimas to their ancestors

who built the casas grandes, the Pima are clearly the inheritors of the ancient Hohokam riverine social and cultural tradition.

In the late 15th or early 16th century, many Yuman-speaking people from what is now southern California seem to have migrated eastward into the lower Colorado River valley. They had been living around the shore of a lake in the basin where the Salton Sea is today. The lake water evaporated, forcing the people to find new territories. The new arrivals apparently began fighting over natural resources with the Indians already in the region. When the Spanish sailor Fernando de Alarón explored the lowest stretch of the Colorado River

Pottery made about 400–600 years ago by artisans of the Hohokam culture, from whom the Pima are probably descended. From left to right: *a human figure found at Snaketown; a female figure from Sacaton; a sheep figure, also from Sacaton.*

in 1540, he reported that the natives were constantly fighting one another. Warfare involving armies of hundreds of men may have begun not long before.

In 1604, Spaniards from New Mexico explored the lower Colorado River. They described the Mojave who lived in the Mojave River valley. Another ethnic group lived between the Mojave and the Quechan (a Yuman-speaking tribe) at the junction of the Gila and Colorado rivers. The Spanish came to refer to them as "Cocomaricopa," their spelling of the Pima word *Kokmalik O'p*, which means "enemies at Big Mountain." In the 1690s, when Catholic missionaries explored the Gila and lower Colorado rivers, constant warfare had forced the Cocomaricopa to settle along the· Gila River west of its great bend. The Quechan still held the Gila-Colorado junction area. Another group, the Cocopah, lived in the rich delta bordering the Gulf of California. Kahwan and Halyikwamai lived between the Cocopah and the Quechan.

In the 1740s a Spanish priest followed native guides along a desert trail from Agua Caliente on the lower Gila River to the Cocomaricopa people who lived on the Colorado River between the Quechan and Mojave. These people called themselves *Halchidhoma* (Outlying People), which the Spaniards wrote as *Jalchedunes*.

In the 1770s another missionary explored even farther. Friar Francisco Garcés found a land route to California via the Yuma (Quechan) Crossing of the Colorado River. He visited Mojaves, ventured east to Hopi Oraibi Pueblo, and went west to the Pacific Ocean and back. Garcés described the opposing alliances and counted the populations that he met. He estimated that the Kahwan, Halyikwamai, and Cocomaricopa (including the Halchidhoma and *Kavelchedom*, or "South People," located along the lower Gila River) numbered 10,000.

Quechans continued attacking Cocomaricopa rancherias with large armies. Stretched in scattered villages from east to west along the lower Gila River, the Kavelchadom could not mobilize rapidly enough to defeat the Quechan. Consequently, they retreated upstream.

Sometime between the 1740s and the 1770s, the Kavelchadom united with the Piman-speaking River People. The groups agreed to defend one another against enemy attack. The farming Pima imposed the condition that the Maricopa hunt less, to reduce competition over hunting grounds. The Pima, numerically larger, left the Maricopa free to follow their own beliefs. The agreement also established an evenly divided council to settle disputes over booty won in battle. Thus, two peoples who spoke different languages created the powerful Pima-Maricopa Confederation. Spanish, Mexican, and eventually U.S. authorities would have to reckon with this force in the region for years to come. ▲

A Maricopa village in an 1859 engraving. The non-Indian artist has mistakenly shown the domed houses with rounded roofs, instead of the flat roofs that were customary.

2

DEFENDING AMERICANS

In 1781, Quechan warriors destroyed two Spanish colonies in their territory and thereby closed the Yuma Crossing. Mexico gained its independence from Spain in 1821, and soon afterward its frontier officials began to employ Cocomaricopa to serve as messengers between the state of Sonora and the California territory. This cooperation angered the Mojave and Quechan, who mobilized their ancient alliance and marched against the Cocomaricopa. In 1827 a Mojave army forced the Halchidhoma away from the Colorado River. The refugees fled to Magdalena, Mexico, where many died in the cholera epidemic of 1832. The following year, survivors traveled north again to join their Kavelchadom relatives on the Gila River.

Quechan and Mojave warriors forced the Kahwan and Halyikwamai into semislavery. Those who survived fled up the Gila River. By 1849, according to the Maricopa who served as interpreter for the commanding general of the Pima-Maricopa Confederation, there were 1,000 Cocomaricopas. If his estimate and that made in 1776 by Francisco Garcés were both correct, nine-tenths of the Cocomaricopa population had died in less than 75 years. The interpreter stated that the Pima were 10 times as numerous as the Maricopa in 1849, numbering 10,000.

The U.S. Army first officially contacted the Pima-Maricopa Confederation in 1846, during the first year of the Mexican War. Brigadier General Stephen W. Kearny led the small Army of the West southwest from Fort Leavenworth, Kansas, into Mexico's Province of New Mexico. Kearny stationed troops in New Mexico towns to protect them from hostile Indian raiders. Then he led his command down the Rio Grande, turning westward to the Gila River. Following the stream through Apache territory early in November, Kearny's army met a Maricopa man looking for his cattle in a pasture east of the Pima villages.

Kearny's quartermaster traded with Pima and Maricopa for food and grain. The Army of the West needed food for men and beasts if it was to reach Mex-

Brigadier General Stephen W. Kearny, who in 1846 led the Army of the West into the Gila River region to negotiate an alliance with the Pima-Maricopa Confederation.

ican California in any condition to fight. Looking ahead, General Kearny worked out an alliance with Confederation general Juan Antonio Llunas. (For administrative purposes, non-Indians gave Spanish or English names to many Pima and Maricopa, and for convenience historians have generally referred to the Indians by these names.) Kearny entrusted worn-out army mules to Llunas "to recruit," or care for, so they could regain their strength, until

Lieutenant Colonel Philip St. George Cooke's battalion arrived on its way to fight in California. Mules were a prime target of Yavapai and Apache raiders, and General Llunas knew that by caring for the mules, the Confederation would be allying itself with the United States against those hostile groups. In making such an alliance, Llunas also knew, the Confederation endangered the one it had concluded with Mexico by treaty in 1823.

Kearny's army had hardly disappeared on the desert trail westward when a messenger arrived from Mexican captain Antonio Comadurán, commander of the military post at Tucson. Comadurán demanded that the Confederation hand over the mules left by the U.S. troops. General Llunas replied that if Mexican troops came after the mules, the Pima-Maricopa Confederation would oppose force with force. No doubt he knew that Comadurán lacked sufficient troops to challenge the Confederation's army. Furthermore, Mexico's frontier forces depended upon the Confederation to help repel Apache raiders. The Tucson garrison even depended on wheat grown by the Pima and Maricopa for its own rations. Secure in the knowledge that the Mexicans needed the help of his forces, Llunas effectively resisted Comadurán's demand and maintained his people's two alliances.

Over the next 15 years, the United States was as dependent upon the Confederation's military might as Mexico

had been. In 1848 the Treaty of Guadalupe Hidalgo ended the war between
Mexico and the United States. Mexico
ceded to the victorious nation most of
its northern territory: present-day California, Arizona north of the Gila River,
most of New Mexico, and portions of
Colorado, Utah, and Nevada. Both
countries set up boundary commissions
to survey the new international frontier. U.S. and Mexican officers surveyed
the new boundary from San Diego, California, to the mouth of the Gila River,
up the Gila, and to the Rio Grande
north of El Paso, Texas.

By 1849, when the gold rush
brought adventurers to the new western lands of the United States, the Pima
were raising not only horses, mules,
and cattle but also poultry domesticated
in the Old World. One forty-niner
called the household where he purchased three chickens for one dollar
"very extra." He and his messmates enjoyed a "first rate dinner."

Mexicans living to the south at-
tended an annual Pima-Maricopa Confederation trade fair. When the
commanding general gave the word to
begin trading, Mexicans sought three
things: great quantities of wheat, numerous cotton sheets, and many baskets made of willow and devil's-claw.
Well-made Pima baskets are watertight,
which made them highly desirable in
the days before metal containers
reached the Sonoran desert peoples.
Thus, women who wove sheets and
baskets profited from two of the three

A Pima woman weaving a large grain-stor-
age basket, photographed in the early 1900s.

major Confederation exports. With the
arrival of the forty-niners, Pima men
and women would profit from trade in
their produce as well as their crafts.

One mess group alone obtained 13
bushels of maize and wheat from Pima
vendors. The grain sustained them
across the desert to the Pacific Coast, as
they had to abandon all of their vehicles
except one light wagon pulled by six
small mules. This group's experience
typified the forty-niners' fortunes on
the Southern Wagon Road to the goldfields. Friendly Pima and Maricopa who
shared their harvests enabled even the
travelers who underestimated their
food needs to reach California.

Had Pima and Maricopa not traded provisions to forty-niners and rescued many of them, many migrants would have died before reaching California. Had hostile Indians, rather than the Pima and Maricopa, occupied the Gila River valley oasis, few of the 20,000 forty-niners who traveled the Southern Wagon Road would have lived to drink Gila River water. As it was, many adventurers did not even survive as far as the oasis.

On August 23, for example, the Little Rock company of forty-niners was in mourning. Young Dr. William P. Fagan had been carried in a wagon for the 50 dry miles north of Tucson, suffering from heat exhaustion. He had begun to bleed from the nose and mouth the night before, and he died early that morning. Fagan's messmates buried him under a large mesquite tree in the desert. Tears ran down the cheeks "of some who I believe never shed a tear before," as they prayed over the grave, wrote one of the group.

The saddened migrants spent another night in the area. A servant died the following day and was buried 100 yards from Fagan. The company then mustered its energies and crossed 25 more desert miles to the Gila River. There the travelers traded with the Pima for enough grain to last until they reached California.

Pima and Maricopa did much more for migrants than feed them. Their Confederation protected travelers from attacks by Apache and other Indians who depended in part on raiding for their subsistence. Some travelers became aware of Confederation military operations; others did not.

On June 6, for example, forty-niners in the area saw columns of smoke rising in the distance. Roadside merchants told them that about 200 Pimas and Maricopas had just returned from a campaign with 6 scalps and 25 women and children. A week later, a migrant who had been at a Pima village reported that an army returned "from a short excursion against the Apaches" with 30 scalps and 2 prisoners.

In mid-July a forty-niner observed about 40 women and children prisoners among the Maricopa. He called them "Apaches," though that term really meant "enemy," and the captives could have been Yavapai or Quechan. Later that month a migrant reported meeting 300 Maricopas some 40 miles up the Gila River on the way home from a battle they claimed to have won. The writer expressed surprise that none of their arrow wounds was bleeding.

In early October a traveler camped opposite Agua Caliente on the lower Gila River counted 150 Maricopa women toting supplies for a like number of warriors carrying weapons. They trudged downstream toward Quechan country. Later that month another traveler noted that a Pima party retaliated against "Apaches" for depredations on Pima-Maricopa livestock, killing 15 to 20 "enemies" and bringing back a number of captives.

Also in mid-October, a Quechan army left the Colorado River, bound for Confederation territory. It returned a few weeks later with two captive boys who were later sold to Mexican slave traders. A Maricopa task force bent on revenge attacked Quechan villages on the east bank of the Colorado at about 4:00 A.M. on October 30. The Quechan fled across the river, losing one man.

The Pima carved symbols into long, thin, wooden rods to help them recall a memorized account of important events. According to Pima record rods, the Confederation's militia met three Apache raiders that autumn. Pima surrounded and killed the raiders on a hilltop, losing one defender. These Apache were probably the thieves reported by a forty-niner as having driven off a horse and two oxen on November 17.

Forty-niners' journals make the half year from June 1 to November 30, 1849, the best-documented period of Confederation warfare. The migrants' writings are especially important because they noted offensives, whereas Pima record rod keepers recorded only enemy raids. During this six-month period, the Confederation conducted at least six major offensives and suffered at least three raids by relatively small parties. If these six months were representative, the Confederation averaged one offensive per month and turned back a raid every other month. The 1849 records are also important because they describe the size of Confederation offensive armies. These ranged from 150 to 300 warriors.

The 1849 accounts hint at the Confederation's military strategy. Descriptions of more than 30 persons killed and captured during an offensive suggest that Confederation forces targeted the Yavapai and Apache camps. They usu-

The record rod, a piece of wood with carved notches to help a storyteller recall specific dates and events in tribal history. These examples are each about 11½ inches long.

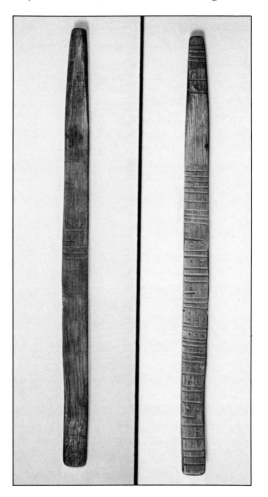

ally attacked the camps nearest the wagon road, which went north from Tucson to the Gila River before turning westward along the river's south bank. Survivors of such assaults probably retreated from Confederation lands, leaving the wagon road safe for travel.

The armies of the Confederation took a high toll of enemies. A record rod account of an 1851 Quechan attack on the Maricopa villages indicates that the Confederation decisively turned back the invaders, injuring or killing 134 Quechans. After the battle, the tra-

John R. Bartlett, U.S. boundary commissioner, sought the aid of the Pima-Maricopa Confederation to rescue the Oatman girls.

ditional purifying rite was held: Women, warriors, and finally young boys danced in concentric circles around trophies of slain enemies in the Confederation's victory celebration.

In 1852, U.S. boundary commissioner John R. Bartlett came up the Gila River from California with his team to the Maricopa villages to seek the Confederation's military and diplomatic assistance. He pitched his largest tent and met with Confederation general Culo Azul and five other chiefs, along with two interpreters, to ask for their aid in rescuing two teenage Mormon girls who had been kidnapped by Yavapai the year before. The girls were Olive and Mary Oatman, who were traveling with their parents and five brothers and sisters to California. Overtaken near the Gila River, the girls watched as their parents and four siblings were clubbed to death and another brother was left for dead. They were captured and marched to the Yavapai village, where they worked as slaves until they were sold to the Mojave. Mary later died during a famine. Quechan efforts to maintain cordial relations with U.S. troops in the area prompted a Quechan leader to persuade Mojave chiefs to release Olive.

The next year, raiders from the Pima-Maricopa Confederation did penetrate Yavapai territory far enough to reach the rancheria where the Oatman girls had been held. Confederation forces effectively continued their conflict with the Quechan-Mojave allies.

Olive Oatman, center, survived a Yavapai attack on her family as they crossed the Sonoran desert in 1857. She and her sister were kept as slaves by the Yavapai, then sold to the Mojave. The Pima-Maricopa Confederation, which at the time protected non-Indians, later avenged her by raiding the kidnappers.

On September 1, 1857, an army of Quechan, Mojave, and Yavapai forces crossed the Agua Fria River and headed east. The invaders surprised a group of Maricopa women who were collecting mesquite pods and killed them all. Runners summoned reinforcements from upstream villages, while the invaders ate the breakfast that the women had been preparing. All day the Maricopa and Pima warriors arrived for what would be known as the Battle of Maricopa Wells. Many years later, Mojave oral history said that the Yavapai retreated after losing only 7 men, but that the Mojave themselves had lost 60 before retreating.

A supervisor of the company that carried mail through the area wrote a brief eyewitness account. He watched the end of the battle from the shade of a nearby mesquite tree. "Besides warriors on foot, every Indian that could get a horse was in the fight," he wrote. War horses proved to be tactically decisive: Mounted Pima men killed a reported 94 Quechans, wiping out the unmounted invading forces.

The 1857 Battle of Maricopa Wells was decisive. After that, the Quechan lacked sufficient warriors to engage in offensive campaigns, and never again did they intrude into Pima-Maricopa territory. Two years later, a U.S. Army task force defeated Mojave warriors in their home valley. The 1857 and 1859 battles ended an era of intergroup warfare waged since prehistoric times.

Politicians in the southern United States were not content with an international boundary set at the Gila River after the Mexican War. The nation was building railroads that would span the continent. Divisions between the southern and northern states over slavery and related issues were sharpening, and southerners wanted a railroad route through the Southwest to connect them to the Pacific Coast. James Gadsden, who supported the southern rail route, became minister to Mexico in 1853. He negotiated the purchase of about 30,000 square miles of land running in a strip west of the Rio Grande and south of the Gila River. He and the Mexicans signed the Gadsden Treaty at the end of 1853; the Senate ratified it late in June 1854. Thus the United States formally acquired land on which the Southern Pacific Railroad would later be built.

As a result of the Gadsden Purchase, the Pima and Maricopa no longer lived partially in territory claimed by Mexico—the United States now asserted sovereignty over their homeland. Two offices of the U.S. government would thenceforth have to deal with them. The Department of the Interior was the new government agency charged with supervising relations with Indians through its Bureau of Indian Affairs (BIA). The BIA operated directly through supervisors known as Indian agents, who were assigned to a tribe or region to carry out government pro-

The first page of the Gadsden Treaty of 1853, by which Mexico transferred to the United States the strip of land that is now southern Arizona. Pima and Maricopa lands thereby came under U.S. jurisdiction.

General William H. Emory, whose 1846 journal provided Americans with their first knowledge of the Pima. In 1853, while a major, he was responsible for explaining to the Indians their rights under the switch from Mexican to U.S. sovereignty.

grams and policy. The other agency was the Department of War, in charge of all U.S. military forces and operations. There were U.S. Army garrisons at El Paso, Texas, and Camp Yuma, California. But the only force capable of defending travelers along the more than 500 miles of road between those posts was the Confederation's army.

William H. Emory was now a major and, as the new U.S. boundary commissioner, was in charge of surveying the new border with Mexico. On June 30, 1855, he was camped at Los Nogales, near where the border crosses the Santa Cruz River, when he was visited by a large delegation from the Confederation. General Azul and the village captains asked Major Emory what the status of their rights would be under the Gadsden Treaty. Emory assured them that whatever rights the Confederation had under Mexican law would be equally upheld by the United States.

Emory asked the general and the captains to continue, in his words, "defending the territory against the savage Apaches" as they had in the past until the federal government could send officials to take over. U.S. troops did not enter the Gadsden Purchase until November 1856, about 17 months after the conference. During those months, the United States was completely dependent on the Confederation to protect its traveling citizens. When the troops finally did arrive, their commander set up his garrison south of Tucson, near the new boundary.

At the end of October 1857, Major Enoch Steen joined John Walker, the first Indian agent sent to the new territory, to request the Confederation's military services. A private company was under contract to the Post Office Department to carry mail between San Antonio, Texas, and San Diego, California. (One witness to the Battle of Maricopa Wells was an employee of this company.) Several heavily armed men guarded mail carried in wagons through the Apachería (Apache territory). West of Tucson, however, only three guards were needed because the Confederation's military protection made the way safe.

Now Major Steen and Agent Walker requested that the Confederation guard the mail for 100 miles south from its territory to Fort Buchanan, plus 100 miles eastward into the Apachería. The Confederation agreed and asked for 500 guns, proposing to conduct a strategic offensive to destroy Apache raiding ability. Major Steen recommended that the government furnish the guns. He calculated that with these arms the Confederation's army would be equivalent to the best mounted regiment in the U.S. Army. The relatively small cost of the guns, Steen claimed, would save the nation hundreds of thousands of dollars annually. Federal officials turned down the request.

In 1858 the U.S. government began treating the Confederation with a mixture of good intentions and callous greed. That year the Butterfield Overland Mail Company (one of the largest private companies yet formed in the country) became the new mail contractor between the Mississippi River and the Pacific Coast. Its stagecoaches were to travel the Gila River road, stopping to change horses and drivers at relay stations to be set up at points along the way.

Congress had authorized the Butterfield Company to choose for itself 320 acres supposedly owned by the government around each of its relay stations. Yet the United States had neither purchased nor conquered any land belonging to the Confederation. Officials of the Interior and War departments recognized that the United States depended on the Pima-Maricopa Confederation to protect the mail company and its passengers against enemy Indians. Some of them also recognized that the land requirements of the mail company threatened the government's military alliance with the Confederation.

A federal special agent who crossed the region in 1858, Godard Bailey, called the Confederation the only barrier against an Apache tide that would flood western Arizona. He officially recommended that the government provide arms to the Confederation, send presents to reaffirm the alliance, and guarantee to the Confederation some of its own lands to avoid intrusions and conflicts that would endanger the alliance. Bailey's superiors, the commissioner of Indian affairs and the secretary of the interior, approved his recommendations, and in February 1859, Congress appropriated $10,000 for guns and presents. However, Special Agent Sylvester Mowry, who was charged with delivering the presents, refused to buy guns, although in 1857 he himself had recommended arming the Confederation. He claimed that freight charges on heavy guns would be too "great a portion of the sum appropriated" and that in any case the Confederation was "almost invariably

Coaches of the Butterfield Overland Mail Company were frequently attacked by the Apache and other hostile tribes in the 1860s and 1870s as they carried mail and passengers between Texas and California. At the request of the U.S. Army, the Pima-Maricopa Confederation protected stagecoach travelers as well as settlers in the region.

successful over their hereditary enemies, the Apaches, with the arms they already possessed."

Congress also appropriated $1,000 to pay a surveyor to establish boundaries for a reservation where the Indians were to live. Mowry estimated the Pima-Maricopa population at about 6,000. Commissioner of Indian Affairs Charles Mix and the House Indian Affairs Committee calculated that 40 acres should be reserved for each person, 240,000 acres in all. The Senate amended the bill to establish the reservation, however, cutting the reserved area by almost three-quarters, to 64,000 acres.

After seeing the bill through the House of Representatives, Representative A. B. Greenwood became commissioner of Indian affairs. As such, he ordered Mowry to inform officials of the mail company that it could not claim ownership of the 320-acre tracts it used within the reservation. Mowry reported that he had obeyed these instructions.

Mowry recruited A. B. Gray, who had earlier surveyed railroad routes, to define the reservation's boundaries. Gray thought that the mail company's operations posed a clear threat to the Pima's irrigated fields and canals. So he chose for the reservation an area within which the irrigation works and fields would be protected from travelers.

The Pima cleared fields and excavated irrigation canals and ditches within a mesquite tree forest that grew two miles north and south of the Gila. Gray laid out a reservation 4 miles wide on a north-south axis, with one offset section jutting out halfway along the 25-mile-long east-west axis. He located the eastern boundary just east of where the Tucson wagon road met the river. Left outside the reservation's eastern boundary were one Pima village and the Little Gila main canal heading. Left outside the western boundary, 25 miles downstream, were all Maricopa villages, fields, and canals.

The mail company hired Silas St. John to encourage Pima and Maricopa farmers to sell him all the grain needed to feed the company's horses. St. John persuaded the Bureau of Indian Affairs to appoint him special agent to represent the government in dealings with

Ammi White, a settler, built this gristmill in the 1850s at what was then called Pima Villages, near the Gila River; he later added a trading post to service mail coaches and travelers. The mill, for turning grain to flour, used water diverted from the river.

the Indians. He distributed some agricultural implements sent by the superintendent of Indian affairs of New Mexico and aided Mowry by handing out other goods to the Indians.

The stagecoach relays led to an increase in travel through the area, and that increase encouraged a settler, Ammi White, to set up an Indian trading post at the "Pima Villages." White, who dealt in grain as well as livestock, invested in a gristmill to turn the raw grain into usable flour. The mill was powered by a waterwheel driven by water from the Gila River.

Civil war split the United States in 1861. The Union called on all forces at its disposal in its contest with the Confederate States of America, and it moved loyal troops from bases in the West to the combat areas in the eastern states. Now only the Pima-Maricopa army and some warriors of the Papago tribe (a Piman-speaking people living just to the south) prevented enraged Apache and hostile Yavapai from robbing Tucson and the Mexican state of Sonora.

Union leaders raised a large volunteer force in California to fight Texan sympathizers of the Confederate states. Crossing the future state of Arizona en route to the Rio Grande, the forward troops of the "Column from California" reached Pima Villages on May 4, 1862. The volunteers were in dire need of feed grains, food for troops, and charcoal for blacksmith operations to put repaired metal rims back on wooden

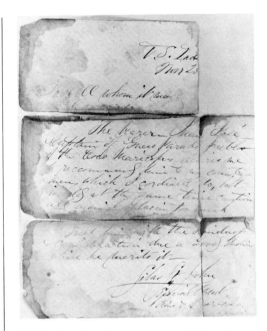

This letter of safe conduct was written by an Indian agent, Silas St. John, for Juan Jose, a Pima village captain, in 1859. Such letters spoke of the longstanding good relations enjoyed between newcomers and the Pima and Maricopa.

wagon wheels that had shrunk in the desert heat. Yet their commander, Lieutenant Colonel Joseph R. West, complained that he had "nothing but promises to offer them in payment"—neither cash nor trade goods with which to pay for provisions. The Pima-Maricopa leaders arranged for the column to buy 143,000 pounds of wheat on credit. After the column moved to New Mexico, the Union relied on the Confederation to protect its very long and vital supply line to the Pacific Coast from hostile Indians.

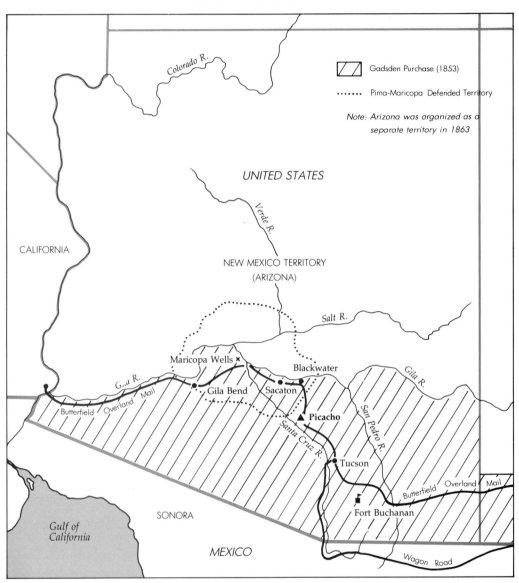

In 1863, Confederation guards sounded an alarm when they saw mounted men approaching from the north. The strangers, however, turned out to be not Yavapai raiders but U.S. citizens seeking provisions. These customers came from the highlands around Prescott, where they had recently discovered gold. The miners had founded camps in the heart of Yavapai country, and the Yavapai expressed their resentment of this intrusion by raiding the mining camps. Their thefts of goods and horses soon led to open warfare, which would alter the old balance of power: Yavapai fighting U.S. citizens became too busy in their homeland to harass the Confederation. The Pima and Maricopa were, therefore, able to take the offensive against the Yavapai.

The miners brought changes beyond the military sphere of life by shipping gold to market. Desperate for precious metals, Union officials acted quickly to ensure the miners' loyalty. Congress created Arizona Territory, and President Lincoln named the territorial officials. In 1864 the first territorial capital was established at Prescott. Early that year, Union troops were stationed at nearby Fort Whipple.

California Volunteers regarrisoned Fort Mojave in 1863. The California Column garrisoned Tucson and Camps Bowie and Grant. The Union built up its military strength in Arizona Territory, but its power was not yet used. The volunteers seldom left the comfort of garrison life to campaign against the militant and dangerous Apache. It was up to the miners and the warriors of the Pima-Maricopa Confederation to carry on the fight against hostile Indians. ▲

When the railroad came to Pima territory in 1879, it signaled an increase in tension between the region's original inhabitants and the newcomers.

COMBINED MILITARY OPERATIONS

From the early 1860s the Pima-Maricopa Confederation aided the embattled Union forces. It did so for the rest of the Civil War and long afterward. In 1865, Brigadier General John Mason led more California Volunteers into Arizona and sent several units into Yavapai country. He set up his own headquarters on the Gila River, sending two companies to establish Camp McDowell on the Verde River just above its junction with the Salt River. The volunteers constructed ramshackle dwellings but did not seek encounters with the Yavapai. Mason wrote that he was not surprised that "the mere establishment of posts in the vicinity of the settlements [was] of no practical importance," because the volunteers "expected hourly to be ordered home" and were reluctant "to make long scouts" in the midst of a severe winter. Major General Irvin McDowell, commander of the Military Department of the Pacific and for whom the camp was named,

reported to the secretary of war that warfare against the Apache called for a more energetic style of soldiering than the volunteer troops could perform.

Territorial governor John N. Goodwin recruited Arizona Volunteers, including one Pima and one Maricopa company. They were mustered into federal duty, serving under non-Indian officers who were citizens of the territory. (The exception was shaman-chief Juan Chevería, captain of the Maricopa company.) Formally attached to Camp McDowell, the Pima and Maricopa volunteers were assigned to Maricopa Wells. Here they not only guarded the Southern Wagon Road and its travelers but also took the offensive against marauding Indian bands.

Commanding the Pima company was John D. Walker, who, as a California Volunteer, had been assigned to Pima Villages to speed up grain purchases for the Union. Reportedly of Great Lakes–area Huron Indian ancestry, Walker was said to ride into action with the Pima company clad in a Pima breechclout. Confederation general Antonio Azul (son of Culo Azul) served with the Pima company and probably led it on campaign. Walker reported briefly that on March 31, 1866, his company had engaged in combat, "killing twenty-five Apaches, taking sixteen prisoners and eight horses. Had three Pimas wounded, one of whom died on the 1st." Walker's force in that battle was almost 400 troops, far larger than any Yavapai or Apache band it attacked.

Before the Arizona Volunteers had completed their one-year enlistment period, troops from the regular "Indian-Fighting Army" (as it was popularly known) returned to western posts. Their commanders were Civil War veterans, confident military professionals. They had fought the first industrial-era war, which was characterized by larger armies than had ever fought before and by railroad transport of men and sup-

Hikers examine bones of some of the 52 Yavapais killed in a canyon near the Salt River by a task force composed of soldiers of the U.S. Army and members of the Pima-Maricopa Confederation. This photograph was taken about 1885.

plies. Army officers, like other veterans who were elected to Congress or were working in the executive branch of government, believed that national might was invincible and "right." This mindset was intolerant of Indian rights, even those of so staunch an ally as the Pima-Maricopa Confederation.

Army enlisted men, after the war, were unlike their officers in most ways. They were, typically, unemployed city men unable to find other work; many were recent immigrants from Ireland, Germany, and other European nations. Like their officers, however, these newest immigrants would fight to conquer still-independent natives and seize their lands.

In 1866, Captain George Sanford led E Troop, First Cavalry, into Camp McDowell. Sanford forged E Troop's recruits into one of the army's most effective Indian-fighting units by leading his men into the field as often as possible. General Antonio Azul observed this aggressive campaigning with approval. After a large Confederation offensive, Azul called upon Sanford to offer his cooperation. Thus began combined military operations by the Confederation and army units at Camp McDowell. These joint offensives peaked in 1868–69, while Brevet Brigadier General Andrew J. Alexander was commander at Camp McDowell.

General Azul led the Confederation's forces, campaigning alongside small contingents under Alexander and his men. As they shared combat, Azul and Alexander formed a friendship. Alexander's wife, Evaline, a devout Presbyterian, had accompanied him to Camp McDowell. Through family connections, she had influence among leaders in eastern states. Pima and Maricopa warriors assembling at Camp McDowell to start a campaign during every full moon caught Evaline's attention. She began a religious women's movement that led to Presbyterian funding of a full-time missionary among the Pima and Maricopa.

While aggressive campaigns largely kept General Azul and his contemporaries busy, other events occurred that would determine the future of the Pima and Maricopa. In 1866 former Major Levi Ruggles became agent for the two tribes. Ruggles soon moved up the Gila River to lead other settlers in founding the town of Florence and initiating a vast canal-building project. The town's residents diverted water from the river in disregard of the Pima and Maricopa's traditional water rights. By 1867 several hundred settlers in Florence were deliberately diverting water onto the desert so that it could not flow down the channel to the Indians. Some wanted to starve the prosperous Indians so they would be forced to work the settlers' fields. Ruggles did not oppose these practices.

Not every federal official was as callous as Ruggles. The superintendent of Indian affairs for Arizona Territory, George W. Leihy, recognized that the reservation's boundaries as set in 1859 did not protect the headwaters leading into the Little Gila Canal, Blackwater Village, and Blackwater Slough from settlers. In 1866, Leihy took steps to enlarge the reservation's boundaries by posting notices that would reserve for the Pima and Maricopa the main Confederation canal and the easternmost village. He advised would-be trespassers that the area was not available for purchase or homesteading. As he returned by stagecoach to his headquarters after posting these notices, Leihy and his clerk were murdered, reportedly by Yavapai.

With Leihy dead, Ruggles reported the postings to Washington, urging that the posted area be reserved. Because the president did not act, the Confederation had to protect its own resources. Part of its army now moved to occupy a zone east of the reservation to prevent settlers from seizing land, canals, and water. Settlers complained to commanders at Camp McDowell, who occasionally sent small detachments to encamp between the Indian army and the settlers to prevent conflict. The army officers did not want to offend General Azul and the village captains. They knew that advancement of their own careers depended on having success against the Apache and Yavapai, and that in turn depended upon continued cooperation with the Confederation.

The Camp McDowell commanders knew, moreover, that the Pima-Maricopa Confederation's army outnum-

Officers and their families at Fort Mc-Dowell, near the Salt River, in 1865. This was the main U.S. Army outpost in Pima-Maricopa lands.

bered any force they could muster. General Alexander himself proved the point after some former officers of the Confederate states charged the Pima with stealing cattle that had actually strayed. Alexander set out with troops and tried to awe the Pima into turning the cattle over to a drover. A Pima captain, Kihau Chinkum, mobilized an army larger than Alexander's unit, so Alexander prudently rode back to camp.

Friction reached a critical point in 1868. The Gila River flooded, destroying three Pima villages, the Sacaton and Casa Blanca trading posts, and the Casa Blanca steam flour mill. Probably hard hit by floodwaters, Pima and Maricopa warriors seized settlers' crops to feed their families.

The dangerous situation in 1867–68 brought no action from the federal Indian peace commission that was journeying across the Plains to arrange land transfers and peace with many native groups. The commission carried out the last flurry of U.S. treaty negotiations with other Indians but ignored the Confederation. So it was that the United States never made a treaty with its loyal ally, the Pima-Maricopa Confederation.

When Ulysses S. Grant became president in 1869, he appointed a Seneca Indian named Ely Parker commissioner of Indian affairs. Parker, who had been Grant's military secretary during the Civil War, appointed many veteran officers from the Union army as Indian agents. One of them, Captain Frederick E. Grossman, arrived in 1869 at Gila River Reservation. He quickly caused a crucial change in Pima-Maricopa well-being: Grossman brought in a physician to vaccinate hundreds of Indians against smallpox, which was then raging in Arizona Territory and northern Mexico and which had decimated the Indians in the past. The Pima and Maricopa population began to grow as a result.

To assert civilian control over Indian affairs, Congress hastened to outlaw Parker's attempt to place army officers in civilian jobs. Dedicated to a policy of peace, President Grant asked various Christian denominations to suggest

men to serve as agents. In 1871, J. H. Stout of the Dutch Reformed Church arrived at Sacaton to replace Grossman. The previous year Grossman had hired the Presbyterian missionary Charles H. Cook as the first government-paid schoolteacher. Stout served several years, but Cook stayed for three decades. Most Pima and Maricopa became Presbyterians, at least outwardly. As for school, parents permitted children to decide for themselves whether to attend. Future rewards for study were "not much of an incentive, much less to those Indian lads whose ideas of greatness center on a fast horse, a pair of spurs, and an American rifle," as Stout put it.

President Grant's negotiator, Vincent Colyer, traveled across Arizona Territory in 1871. He arranged peace with the Chiricahua Apache chief Cochise and other Apache leaders and designated reservations for that tribe. Colyer did not think that there was anything for the United States to negotiate with its firm ally, the Pima-Maricopa Confederation. Perhaps because he did not recognize the problems the Confederation was having, he did nothing to protect its traditional water rights from the depredations that were already taking place.

The army commander in Arizona, however, opposed Colyer's efforts and continued hostilities against the Apache. In 1872, President Grant sent a Civil War hero, Major General O. O. Howard, to renegotiate peace with the

Apache. Howard convened a conference with area Indians at Camp Grant. Here General Antonio Azul spoke eloquently, urging Apache leaders to abide by their previous pledge to live peacefully and to obey federal officials. They agreed, and Azul promised that the Confederation would observe the peace and that his people welcomed peaceful relations and friendship with the Apache.

The pacification of the Apache brought a new sense of security to the region, spurring settlers to move farther up the Gila River from the Pima-Maricopa canals. Miners began removing high-grade copper ore at a new camp called Clifton. One businessman hired Mexican-Americans to cut mesquite trees in Safford Valley to make charcoal for fuel in the mines and smelters. In 1872, Mormons arrived in that valley and began diverting Gila River water, utterly disregarding Pima and Maricopa legal rights to those waters under Arizona Territory law.

Even after Major General Howard's 1872 peace conference, the army, suspicious of some tribes, continued to fight the Yavapai and Apache in Arizona Territory and continued to persuade Congress to appropriate funds for military posts. Unlike army officers, the Pima-Maricopa Confederation took seriously the agreements reached in 1871 and 1872. The Confederation ceased its offensives but remained alert in case its military services were needed by the United States or the territory. As late as 1878, the Confederation army rode quickly to the rescue when renegade Apache attacked a wagon train on a road near Florence. In 1886, Pima scouts rode with the U.S. task force that searched for the Chiricahua Apache renegade Geronimo and his followers. When they were brought to bay and Geronimo surrendered, the battles with the Apache were over.

The Confederation's army protected the Little Gila Canal heading and Blackwater Village from settlers until 1876, and perhaps later. In that year, at Major General Irvin McDowell's prompting, President Grant issued an executive order expanding Gila River Reservation. The order added enough land to bring nearly all of the Little Gila Canal, its headwaters, and Blackwater Slough and Village south of the head of the canal within the reserved area. This included almost all the land that Superintendent Leihy had posted 10 years earlier, land on which the Indians were already living. Land one mile farther east, however, containing the main Blackwater alluvial spring in the riverbed, was not included in the order. The Blackwater spring furnished vital irrigation water when surface flow diminished to little or nothing; without it the Pima had less insurance against dry seasons.

General McDowell had used a very telling argument in persuading President Grant to act. Aware of the friction between settlers and Pima in the Blackwater area, McDowell raised the specter

Pima and Maricopa children in front of their school at the Sacaton agency, 1875. At right is J. H. Stout, a missionary who was also the schoolteacher and Indian agent. The children had to wear American-style clothes to school.

of an expensive Indian war if Pima lands and waters went unprotected. Congress was in no mood to appropriate money for the army in that year, in which the centennial of the nation's birth had been marred by the Seventh Cavalry's defeat at the hands of the Sioux on the Little Big Horn.

Grant's 1876 executive order did nothing for the Maricopa, who were not well off. As Gila River water was stolen upstream, both the Pima and Maricopa expanded the pastures and crops that were irrigated from the Salt River. Juan Chevería led inhabitants of Bone Standing Village to downstream fields that were irrigated by canals drawing water from the Salt about five miles above its junction with the Gila. These fields and canals were even farther from the western edge of the 1859 reservation than Bone Standing Village was. General McDowell kept track of the well-being of Juan Chevería and other Maricopa, and he and other officers at Camp McDowell kept up a steady correspon-

Mounted scouts who went into Mexico to find the renegade Apache leader Geronimo in 1886. More than 30 Pima-Maricopa Confederation troops rode with the U.S. Army expedition. Geronimo's surrender ended the Apache rebellion.

dence that emphasized the need for federal protection of Maricopa and Pima land and water rights.

BIA officials may have resisted McDowell's efforts, but they prepared their own contingency plans. A draft executive order was ready when Camp McDowell's commanding officer hit the critical political nerve early in 1879. Reporting that a large number of Mormons had left Utah Territory and were headed for the Salt River valley, he asked whether the government should not protect Pima and Maricopa land and water rights there before the Mormons arrived. On January 10, 1879,

President Rutherford B. Hayes signed an order directing the General Land Office to halt sales of land on the north bank of the Gila River to its junction with the Salt River, and for two miles north and south of the Salt River upstream to the Fort Apache Reservation. The order adequately protected the Confederation's water rights in the Salt River valley as guaranteed by the 1848 Treaty of Guadalupe Hidalgo.

Unfortunately for the Pima-Maricopa people and U.S. national honor, this order was only a temporary measure. It gained time for federal officials to decide how the settlers could use their political power to work around Pima-Maricopa legal rights. Settlers actually had few farms in the Salt River valley early in 1879, but several canal companies were active in the area. Anticipating heavy demand for water from future farmers, they were already excavating giant ditches for canals that they would fill with Salt River water to sell at a high profit. The investor-speculators counted on the Southern Pacific Railroad to transport likely customers to the valley. Railroad crews were laying tracks eastward from the Colorado River as fast as possible early in 1879. By May the desert heat made the steel rails difficult to handle, and the company had trouble getting deliveries from eastern steel mills. The end-of-track point became stalled 13 miles south of Sacaton. The railroad named

the station there "Casa Grande" after the four-story, earthen-walled ancestral Blackwater Pima stronghold.

A few weeks earlier, the railroad had begun train service to the new Maricopa Station on the Gila River Indian Reservation. The first train carried speculators from San Francisco to a town-lot auction at the station. One lot sold for $1,400, sharpening the appetite of Salt River valley speculators for the profits they expected to see when the railroad carried farmers to Maricopa, from where they would continue by stagecoach to the trading center at Phoenix.

The railroad owners and local speculators wielded political power, and they almost succeeded in having the Hayes administration abandon its role as trustee and protector of Confederation land and water rights. In June the

Crews for the Southern Pacific Railroad laying track into Pima territory in 1879, linking Texas with the Pacific Coast. The first train brought farmers and land speculators and gave the trading post of Phoenix its real start as a regional center.

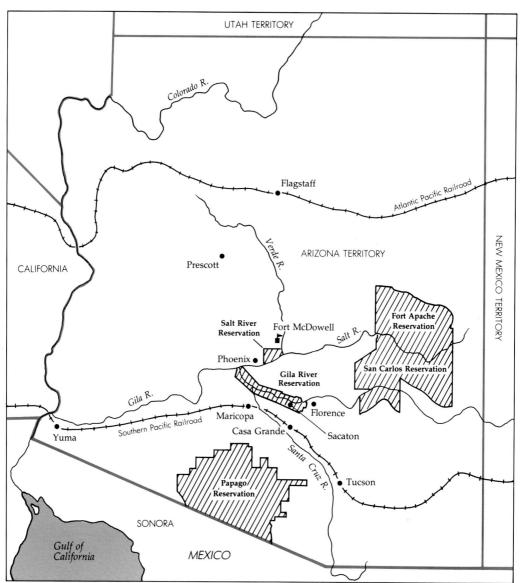

president signed an executive order that retreated far from the January order.

The June order did expand Gila River Reservation in two directions, reserving only minor areas around Pima and Maricopa villages, fields, and canals. It expanded Gila River Reservation to the northwest along the north bank of the Gila River to its junction with the Salt River and then four miles up the Salt. The new boundary then ran southeast to the northeast tip of the 1859 reservation. This extension protected the Maricopa village of Sacate in the Gila and Maricopa Colony on the Salt. It also protected the Indians' fields and most of their canals—but not the colony's main canal.

The June order also created a separate, noncontiguous outpost of Gila River Reservation many miles up Salt River. Now called Salt River Reservation, it is located south of Camp McDowell along the Salt River and includes the site of the main dam that diverted Salt River water into white farmers' irrigation canals. Although the June order reserved some Salt River valley fields and water for Pima and Maricopa, it once more opened most of the riverbank to settlement.

Meanwhile, settlement in the Prescott highlands expanded every year after 1863. Disputes arose over water, and some ended in court. In 1879 the territorial court heard one such case, *Kelsey v. McAteer*. The judge held that anyone's right to use surface-flowing water for irrigation or other "beneficial uses" in Arizona was derived from and depended upon "prior appropriation." Thus the first person to "beneficially" use water from a stream established a right to continue doing so, even in dry years. Later arrivals could gain only "junior," or wet year, rights. This decision became the basic legal principle in an arid region where stream flows vary greatly from year to year.

General McDowell immediately pointed out to his superiors that the Pima and Maricopa people, who had been irrigating for centuries, did indeed have prior-appropriation water rights. He urged prompt court action to enforce those rights. Unfortunately for these peaceful farmers, no other federal officials during McDowell's time shared his enthusiasm for securing those rights. Pima and Maricopa history since 1879 has been a story of the failure of the federal government to go to court to protect their prior-appropriation water rights or to use marshals or the army to stop the theft of that water. Since 1879, federal officials have turned away while the Pima and Maricopa plunged from prosperity into severe poverty.

That plunge occurred because settlers who came into Arizona river valleys in increasing numbers after 1879 took more and more water to irrigate their farms. As anticipated, the railroad contributed to the rapid growth of the non-Indian population. On January 24, 1880, crews began laying track southeast from Casa Grande Station, and on March 20 they finished the line connecting Tucson and the Pacific Coast. In September they crossed the Arizona–New Mexico border, finishing the southern transcontinental route.

In 1870 the Confederation had been the largest ethnic group in Arizona Territory. By 1880, whites were the largest ethnic group, and the white population more than doubled in the next 10 years.

As settlers rushed into the territory, General McDowell and some officials of the Interior Department shared a con-

The agency police of the Gila River Reservation, photographed in 1881. Louis Morago, a hero of the wars with the Apache, is in the second row, second from left.

cern. Some irrigated fields, canals, and villages of the Pima and Maricopa remained outside the reservations. In 1882 the energetic Roswell G. Wheeler, the agent at Sacaton, urged the commissioner of Indian affairs to enlarge Gila River Reservation. Wheeler visited western Pima and Maricopa farmers near Gila Crossing on the Maricopa-Phoenix wagon road and reported that he had seen no finer farms in Arizona. He urged that Pima and Maricopa lands south of the river be added to the reservation. President Chester A. Arthur signed an order adding lands south and west of the Gila to the reservation.

Wheeler's successor, A. H. Jackson, notified the BIA that some Pima winter villages were still outside the reservation and that he could not send agency police off reservation to enforce the law. Moreover, Jackson explained, the Pima and Maricopa needed continued access to desert pasturage for their 13,000 ponies, and he called for further enlargement of the reservation. In 1883, in response to Jackson's request, President Arthur issued another executive order, which added thousands of desert acres to Gila River Reservation.

Despite these efforts, no executive order or other federal action halted the sale of lands upstream to citizens or slowed the rate of upstream water theft. Other federal actions displayed callousness toward Pima and Maricopa welfare. The high rate of European immigration in the 1880s contributed to a national epidemic of tuberculosis. Doctors extolled living in the arid Southwest as a cure. The BIA assigned tubercular employees to western reservations, including Sacaton agency, from which the bacillus that causes the disease spread rapidly among malnourished Pima and Maricopa unable to resist infection. Indian children attending boarding schools in other parts of the country suffered especially high death rates as a result of the radically different climate there. The superintendent at Sacaton concurred: "It is simply murder to send the children to northern and eastern schools," he wrote.

Land and water speculators continued to steal Gila River water between the reservation and the mountains. In 1888 the Florence–Casa Grande Canal Company purchased a huge dragline to excavate a main canal from the river to Picacho Reservoir and on southward to the Casa Grande railroad station. Fed-

General Antonio Azul of the Pima-Maricopa Confederation, photographed in October 1872 wearing a headdress of handwoven cloth. He acted as peacemaker between his people, the Apache, and the U.S. Army, helping to end decades of hostility.

eral authorities failed to halt this grand theft of Pima and Maricopa water. The General Land Office continued selling "desert lands" to speculators who promised to irrigate their fields from the new canal. Yet the Pima and Maricopa continued to teach their children to get along with their new neighbors. ▲

A Pima woman holds a length of split willow in her mouth while making a coiled basket in this photograph from about 1905. A burden basket leans against the domed house, and pottery and other household goods lie on the ground.

POVERTY
AND
DEPENDENCE

In the 1850s the Pima and Maricopa population dropped sharply. From perhaps 11,000 persons in 1850, it fell to less than half that number within a few years. The decline was a result of disease (especially cholera), war, and starvation. The tribes' numbers probably reached a low point in the late 1860s or early 1870s. Then, in 1890, when the local Indian agent took a new count, he found that the Pima and Maricopa population had increased. His count of 4,779 was probably low, the true number being about 5,300.

This small improvement was primarily due to smallpox vaccinations arranged by the Indian agent and to the tribes' ability to adapt to altered conditions. But tuberculosis and malnutrition continued to exact a toll. Winter wheat was the only Gila River Reservation crop that could be irrigated, because water thieves upstream were already taking off so much of the spring and summer flow. Farmers in Maricopa Colony and on the Salt River Reserva-

tion fared better, as the Salt River still flowed near its original level.

Because their food crop was so variable and their old way of life disrupted, the Pima and Maricopa now needed money. They needed it for clothing, because without proper summer water they were unable to grow cotton, their traditional fiber. They needed it for wagons, sugar, coffee, and canned goods, to replace traditional foodstuffs lost ever since whites had settled in their territories. To obtain cash, Pima and Maricopa women, who formerly collected dead mesquite branches for firewood, now sold baskets and pots to non-Indians. Men began cutting down live mesquite trees and selling them in nearby towns. Mesquite roots tap water as deep as 50 feet below the surface, and their leaves enrich the soil. Aware of the trees' value, the BIA forbade the felling of live trees, but poverty forced the Pima and Maricopa to disregard the edict. The Gila River mesquite forest— a major natural resource—shrank.

One of the first bridges across the Gila River, near Florence, shown in 1882. The bridge later washed out.

For decades the federal government did little to improve the desperate condition of the Pima and Maricopa people. Agents' reports to the commissioner of Indian affairs went unheeded. In the mid-1890s intervention arrived in the form of the U.S. Geological Survey. One of the survey's tasks was to help develop agriculture in the West by advising on land and water resources. Its hydrologists, or water experts, were concerned not with the Indians' increasing poverty, however, but with what were known as "conservation" issues. Survey engineers proposed damming streams in order to capture occasional floodwaters for irrigation. Some regarded any water flowing downstream as wasted, for it did not serve any immediate agricultural purpose.

In the late 19th century Congress was not yet convinced that the federal government should pay for development in the West's arid regions. Private enterprise had usually taken the lead in the past, and again investors and speculators came forward. Some of them formed the Hudson Reservoir and Canal Company ostensibly to sell Salt River water. The company obtained title to a dam site near where Tonto Creek joins the Salt River; it planned to expand the recently built canal system in the lower Salt River valley. To move water to lands in the Casa Grande area to the south, the company would need to dig a large canal across Gila River Reservation. Congress approved the heart of the scheme in 1897, authorizing the company to claim a right-of-way across the reservation. There was one restriction: Congress required that the company provide irrigation water to Pima and Maricopa farmers whose fields lay along the proposed canal. The company balked at the added expense and never built the canal.

President Theodore Roosevelt, who took office in 1901, favored expanding the government's role in the West, and his enthusiasm spread to Congress. The notion of a federal role in reclaiming arid western lands gathered speed: High dams on rivers and streams would block, store, and distribute water through canals for irrigation. Congress passed the Federal Reclamation Act in 1902, and the newly established Bureau of Reclamation began to try to reshape the West. The bureau bought the Tonto Creek dam site from the Hudson Reservoir and Canal Company, and, in cooperation with Salt River valley farmers and speculators, survey engineers began in 1903 to build a high dam. The masonry structure was named Theodore Roosevelt Dam.

A few miles to the south, survey engineers were still investigating the Gila River for potential dam sites. In 1900 one of them, Joseph B. Lippincott, recommended damming the river near San Carlos, an Apache hamlet set up by the BIA about 100 miles east of and upstream from Gila River Reservation. With dams planned for both of the region's principal waterways, the process that would forever change the ecology of the region was under way.

If the system worked as the engineers said it would, the Pima and Maricopa farmers would benefit. Supporters of the San Carlos dam testified that it would capture enough floodwater to furnish the people of the Gila River Reservation with enough irrigation water to make their farms fully productive again.

As the dam projects went slowly ahead, a majority of Congress believed that the Maricopa and Pima were worthy former allies who had been deprived by federal neglect of their irrigation water and consequently of the capacity to produce enough food for themselves. Congress was willing, therefore, to appropriate funds to relieve their poverty. Yet it was rarely willing to prod the executive branch into prosecuting specific water rights cases vigorously, so Pima and Maricopa rights to irrigation water went largely unenforced.

It was a rare occasion when any white man with political power spoke up for the Indians. The only lawsuit filed in this period, in fact, resulted from the dedication of Matthew Murphy, a low-ranking BIA employee. Murphy, who worked with farmers at Maricopa Colony, was dismayed when he learned of upstream farmers' plans to dig another canal that would drain the Salt River above the Maricopa Ditch. Cyrus Sun, an educated spokesman for the Maricopa, urged the local government attorney in 1902 to file a suit on behalf of individual Maricopa farmers, because few of them were literate and in any event Indians were not allowed to testify in territorial courts. The attorney did so. Murphy then presented the evidence that established Maricopa rights to the water, and the court decided in their favor. The judge stopped the canal scheme and appointed Murphy to supervise water sharing.

Not only did officials in higher places fail to act with equal energy on behalf of the Indians, some even betrayed their trust. W. H. Code, an engineer for the Indian Irrigation Service (IIS), an arm of the BIA, also worked as vice-president of a bank in the town of Mesa. The bank was run by A. J. Chandler, a major investor and speculator in the southern Salt River valley. At the start of the century, Code launched an ambitious project to irrigate 10,000 acres on the Gila River Reservation with water pumped by electric motors from very deep wells. This technology was still experimental, yet the scheme called for 10 such wells. Code and his cohorts at the Bureau of Reclamation persuaded Congress to appropriate $540,000 for the experiment. One major problem with the scheme was that to farm the pump-irrigated fields, Indian families would have to abandon their existing fenced farms and homes and migrate to the project area. There they would have to clear new fields, learn to farm them, and build new fences, homes, and barns. Even if the experiment had brought 10,000 acres under irrigation—which it never did, because the pumps were not built and there was not enough groundwater anyway—the project area could hold only 2,000 families, each farming a mere 5 acres. At that time, federal law allowed non-Indian homesteaders to claim 160 acres of public domain per person, and many homesteader families had members file on adjoining plots. Thus, the government employee in charge intended to favor non-Indians by a ratio of at least 32 to 1.

Code actually helped draft a bill that revealed his true motive. To pay for the project, the government would sell 180,000 acres from the reservation; Chandler, who had already acquired extensive tracts of adjacent land illegally by using dummy homesteaders, would be the buyer. As amended by Congress, however, the bill permitted the sale of the reservation lands but did not require it. The 180,000 acres stayed in the reservation.

Government actions based on broken promises extended to many fields. In 1907 the Agriculture and Interior departments agreed to set up a new experimental station at Sacaton for growing Egyptian long-staple cotton plants, whose fibers were longer than the short fibers then grown in the United States. For 50 years, plant breeders labored there, on Gila River Reservation, to create new high-yielding varieties. As a result of their efforts, U.S. farmers now grow long-staple cotton for domestic textile mills. From the start, the commissioner of Indian affairs ordered that the project be conducted in secret. The government did not consult the Pima, nor did it pay them for using land, water, and electricity reserved for the Indians by a 1907 contract.

In 1904 greater public awareness of Pima and Maricopa poverty spurred the president to set up a three-man fact-finding panel that included the commissioner of Indian affairs. The trio traveled to reservation villages to record testimony about personal and family life. Many witnesses spoke poignantly of their unwilling economic depen-

(continued on page 73)

WORK IN REED AND CLAY

Pima and Maricopa women have woven baskets and made pottery for centuries. Most wares were functional, serving as storage containers or carrying vessels. As large numbers of non-Indians arrived in Pima territory in the mid-1800s, these crafts changed. The Pima began to weave nonfunctional small baskets to exchange for metal tools and other merchandise with traders and travelers. Similarly, the Maricopa shaped more decorative clay urns and vases. The newer, ornamental pieces often departed from traditional styles, catering instead to the tastes of collectors.

Despite changes in style, materials and methods for weaving and pottery making remained mostly the same. Willow twigs, cattail-reed stems, and the black pods of the Martynia (devil's-claw) plant were pliable when wet, durable when dry. Starting around 1850, Pima basket weavers added glass beads that they received from non-Indian traders. Blue beads were most common, although yellow, white, and red ones occasionally appear, too.

Since World War II, fewer Pima and Maricopa have been making baskets and pots. But those who continue to practice these traditional crafts produce pieces that are among the finest known.

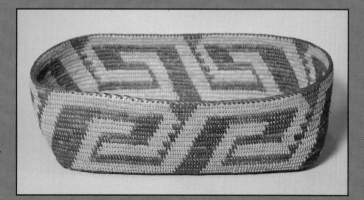

Oblong basket, about 13 inches long and 3 inches high, probably made in the 1950s. Though the shape of this piece is unusual, the materials are traditional.

A variety of Pima baskets. Clockwise from top left: a bowl with 12 figures of women around a black center; a plaque with a large maze design; a bowl with three fields of rain clouds and swastika (which for the Pima symbolizes a whirlwind); a small vase, also with rain cloud symbols; and a large storage vessel with whirlwind designs, made in 1915.

Grace Kisto, one of the most skilled Pima basket makers, wove this abstract plaque in the late 1970s.

Another plaque woven by Grace Kisto in the 1970s. The 12-pointed star is a symbol long used by the Pima.

Plaque with figure designs. From center: four eagles; men, dogs, and coyotes; deer and bighorn sheep; women.

Baskets of simple shape, with intricate beadwork used as edgings or (bottom right) to accentuate the pattern.

Beaded baskets, early 20th century. The one at right includes the name of a brand of coffee popular at the time, Arbuckles.

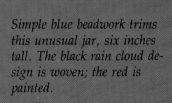

Simple blue beadwork trims this unusual jar, six inches tall. The black rain cloud design is woven; the red is painted.

Three vases and a jar. The shapes and designs of Pima and Maricopa pottery have their origins in the ancient Hohokam culture of what is now the American Southwest.

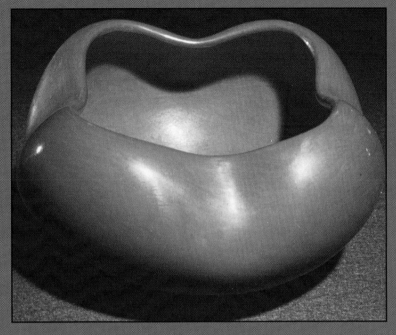

Prize-winning bowl of polished redware, made in the 1950s by Mary Juan, a Pima.

Redware vase with black design, made in the 1960s by Alice Cort.

The design on the black-on-red jar (left) recalls
the Pima's original adobe houses, whereas the
Grecian style of the vase shows the influence of
other cultures on Pima art today.

By 1920, as the local non-Indian economy became based on cash, the Pima sank into poverty. They continued to build traditional houses and their children wore traditional clothing until they entered school.

(continued from page 64)

dency on the government and of the consequences of that dependency.

More than one hardworking Pima described how a widow had starved when her neighbors could no longer deprive their own children of food in order to share with her. A bereaved father testified that his family went off the reservation to buy food. Green (unripe) wheat was the only provision they had for the trip. A young son fell ill during the journey, his malnourished body unable to digest the only food that his parents could provide.

A few young Pima pursued formal education as a path to economic independence. At least one, Lewis D. Nel-

son, had begun teaching in a white school off the reservation in 1897. By 1904 two of the five schoolteachers at Sacaton were local Indian women, but most girls could earn "good wages" as domestic servants "as soon as they leave school," according to a BIA inspector. Most youths, though fluent in English, still attempted to produce food for their families by farming. Very few aspired to be servants.

An era ended for the Pima and Maricopa in 1908 when Antonio Azul, who symbolized their effort to hold on to traditional ways, died. He was the last general of the Pima-Maricopa Confederation. After his death, his already el-

Pima crossing the Gila River on their way to an off-reservation town for food in 1907. By the 1890s their farms had ceased being productive because the water they depended on to irrigate their fields was being diverted by non-Indian settlers.

derly son, Antonito Azul, became chief of the Pima. The title, less resounding than "general," reflected the ebbing of Pima power since the time 50 years earlier when the Confederation had been a real military force. Antonito walked in an increasingly white world, having learned to speak English and to interpret as early as 1879. He and the other people living on the Gila River Reservation recognized that their circumstances had changed. In the 20th century they needed leaders who not only spoke English but also understood law, business, and the workings of the BIA.

In 1911 the people created what they called a "business committee," signal-

ing their new approach to political affairs. Its members were five younger men with formal education—among them Kisto J. Morago, a son of Louis Morago, the Apache Wars hero of the 1860s, and Lewis D. Nelson, the teacher. Nelson had investigated financial fraud committed by the agent at Sacaton, J. P. Alexander. The agent was so angry that he physically attacked Nelson during the Pima year corresponding to 1908–09. That incident and other complaints finally compelled the BIA itself to investigate Alexander, and he was eventually forced to resign.

In 1910 the Reverend Charles H. Cook, the aging Presbyterian missionary, stepped aside in favor of the Reverend Dirk Lay. Lay arrived from an Iowa seminary and quickly became emotionally involved with the problems of the Pima and Maricopa. He spent most of the rest of his life organizing public support for government actions to restore irrigation water to the Indians.

Early in his career at Sacaton, Lay joined with Herbert Marten, a local employee of the BIA. Marten was disgusted by the corruption of Alexander and survey engineer Code. Lay, Mar-

ten, and others persuaded the House Indian Affairs Committee to hold hearings in 1912 on the plight of the Pima and Maricopa. Antonito Azul sent a statement, and Marten presented devastating testimony in which he described Code's failed pumping experiment and his conflict of interest in associating with the land speculator Chandler.

Despite public pressure, Congress took no immediate action on Marten's testimony. Instead, it called for more technical studies by the Army Corps of

General Antonio Azul (center), with his son Antonito, later chief of the Pima, and grandson Harry, photographed about 1900.

Engineers. This group was created within the army to build large, up-to-date water-modification projects. Its funding has depended on its ability to persuade Congress that big new structures such as dams could ease flooding and other problems.

A three-member board of engineers studied Pima and Maricopa water needs and the feasibility of a high dam at San Carlos. In the report, the corps admitted that it knew little of historic Pima and Maricopa irrigation practices or rights. It then estimated that 35,000 acres on Gila River Reservation could be irrigated. In 1914 the corps certified that a dam 200 feet high could indeed be built.

Congress authorized construction of a small diversion dam across the Gila River just downstream from the site originally proposed in 1897. Congress included in this legislation the corps'

estimate of 35,000 irrigable acres on Gila River Reservation. It coupled that area with 27,000 acres of non-Indian lands in the Florence–Casa Grande Project (a canal not finished until the 1920s) that competed for Gila River water.

Very little of the 27,000 acres was ever irrigated. Most of it was owned by the federal government or by speculators, some of whom did not even live in Arizona. The Department of the Interior forged ahead anyway. It devised a "Landowners' Agreement" that the secretary of the interior, acting as trustee for Pima and Maricopa lands, approved. According to this agreement, the Pima would share water diverted at the new dam with non-Indian landowners.

Meanwhile, Arizona had gained statehood in 1912. The diversion dam was named for two of the first legislators the state sent to Washington,

Excavation of the Florence–Casa Grande canal, which by the 1920s was diverting Gila River waters. Workers began with horses and picks but finished with steam-powered machinery.

In the 1910s a hotel owner fooled Congress into paying for this bridge across the Gila River, now mostly dry, by claiming that it was a dam (foreground). Sightseers could walk from the hotel to the Pima monument of Casa Grande.

Senator Henry F. Ashurst and Representative Carl Hayden (son of a pioneer flour miller who had long traded with the Pima). According to the landowners' agreement, the reservation would get between 51.7 and 60.6 percent of the water, depending on the river's flow rate; on average the Pima would receive 56.1 percent of the diverted water. The rest, an average of 43.9 percent, was for non-Indian lands. Yet at no time since the agreement was signed have the Pima received their legal portion of di-

verted water. Year after year, non-Indians have received more than half the diverted flow, according to government records from an official 1985 study.

Despite congressional exposure of his illegal acquisition of homesteaded lands, A. J. Chandler still had influence in high places. Chandler wanted Congress to build a bridge across the Gila River so that guests at his San Marcos Hotel in the desert south of Phoenix could visit the imposing, four-story, earthen-walled Blackwater Village stronghold (now called Casa Grande Ruins National Monument). In the 1910s he persuaded Congress to finance the bridge and then convinced the state to pave the road between hotel and monument. (The BIA disguised the bridge as a second diversion dam to benefit the Pima; in fact, only about 10 percent of the concrete went for the dam.) In an era of slow communication and little government supervision in the West, speculators had no difficulty in concealing their operations from officials in Washington. Eastern congressmen voted for bills that were meant to aid the Pima and Maricopa, usually without knowing that Arizona land speculators were the true beneficiaries.

Startling changes in land-use patterns in the arid West first brought about by dams were increased by the arrival of the automobile. The Pima and Maricopa had only recently entered the age of the horse and wagon. Now, even before every family had a rig for hauling wood to town, autos appeared on the scene. Paved roads soon gave everyone with a car access in an hour to regions that a wagon would reach in a day. Each technological change put added pressure on the Pima and Maricopa to participate in the cash economy, even if that meant abandoning traditional native values.

When money was not a factor, the Pima and Maricopa acted much like their neighbors. For example, after the start of the Mexican Revolution in 1910, Americans along the borders were put on military alert. Young Pima and Maricopa men attending the Indian school in Phoenix organized an Indian Arizona National Guard company. Mexican unrest continued throughout most of the decade, with raiders crossing the border to attack targets in the southwestern United States. When President Woodrow Wilson called the guard into federal service in 1916, the Indian student-soldiers helped protect the border.

In 1917 the United States joined the fight against Germany in World War I and sent troops overseas. Arizona National Guard units that had served on the Mexican border went to France, where the Indian soldiers among them fought bravely in the murderous trench warfare. Matthew Juan, a Pima, was the first Arizona soldier killed in action in France.

Yet bravery overseas could not wipe out injustice at home. With the end of the war on November 11, 1918, Pima and Maricopa veterans returned to Gila River Reservation hoping to be allotted reserved lands under the General Allotment Act (Dawes Act). This act, passed by Congress in 1887, had provided for allotting 160 acres to each Indian head of household, 40 acres to minors, and none to women. Protests from various Indian communities led to an 1891 amendment by which every Indian was to receive 80 acres of farming land or 160 acres of grazing land. Allotment was designed to apportion land fairly to individual farmers, but on the whole the plan is considered to have

The marching band of the Indian school in Phoenix, Arizona, parading before a football game in the early 1900s. Students at the school also organized a National Guard unit that fought in World Wars I and II.

been a failure. It resulted in Indians losing millions of acres of land that had once been reserved for their communal ownership and use.

The BIA never allotted 80 acres to each Maricopa and Pima, even though each member of a non-Indian family that drew Gila River water via the Florence–Casa Grande Project could own 160 acres. Instead, between 1911 and 1923, in a clearly discriminatory move, each Pima and Maricopa received only 20 acres, of which only 10 were supposedly irrigable. The other 10 were called grazing land, which in the desert meant little. Even by pooling their allotted parcels, families could not put together a tract large enough to farm profitably. Nor was water available to irrigate the 10-acre tracts, because the BIA had failed to protect the reservation's water rights in court before it allotted the land.

Now, to provide water as promised, the BIA reluctantly joined an effort to persuade Congress to authorize the high dam at San Carlos proposed long before. This effort was led by Dirk Lay and Presbyterians across the country, who believed that a dam across the Gila River would capture enough floodwater to furnish Gila River Reservation with adequate water. Though Lay meant well, he was deceived by the early success of the Salt River Project and did not realize how quickly non-Indians would steal the new supply. Moreover, supporters of the Gila River high dam overestimated the amount of flood runoff. Those who sympathized with the Maricopa and Pima were seeking a technical solution to what was really a problem of stolen water.

As the truth about the poverty of the Pima and Maricopa reached the East, nationwide pressure, especially from Presbyterians, finally moved Congress in 1924 to authorize the high dam at San Carlos. Representative Hayden en-

sured that the water to be stored by the dam would irrigate an additional 23,000 non-Indian acres as well as 15,546 Gila River Reservation acres. The act forced the Department of the Interior finally to file suit in 1925 to protect reservation water rights against illegal diverters upstream. The case dragged on for 10 years. Meanwhile, the dam was completed and dedicated in 1930 by former president Calvin Coolidge, after whom it is named.

In recognition of the bravery Indians showed in World War I, in 1924 Congress extended citizenship to any In-

Construction of the Coolidge Dam on the Gila River, two years before the dam was completed in 1930. In 1983, when the government prohibited the dam's directors from charging part of the operating costs to the Pima and Maricopa, they turned off its generators.

dian born in the United States who was not already a citizen under other laws. Those Pima and Maricopa who had a formal education and who had already chosen not to live on a reservation did exercise their right to vote, especially after 1924. Despite the new law, state officials tried to prevent Indians on reservations from voting, on the grounds that reservation Indians had the legal status of "wards of the government." By definition, a "ward" was not competent or able to manage his or her own affairs. In 1928 the Arizona Supreme Court upheld that argument, ruling that Indians living on reserved lands could not vote. This technicality propped up the decision, but the ruling was probably motivated by racial discrimination. The Pima and Maricopa had learned to speak fluent English, to read, and to write, and the vote was rightfully theirs. The state supreme court didn't confer that right until 1948.

Slowly, Maricopa and Pima who had learned English were gaining ground. A. H. Kneale, a veteran BIA employee, became superintendent at Sacaton in 1930. As Kneale entered the room for his first community meeting at the Gila River Reservation, he remembered a time earlier in his career when he had seen Pine Ridge Sioux in the Dakotas dancing naked around a fire. Now, "here was something different," Kneale later wrote. "The meeting was being held in one of the numerous day-school buildings that dotted the reservation and had been opened by prayer, in English, by the chairman." Kneale, who had always used an interpreter when addressing Indians, asked the chairman whether he needed one here. The chairman told him to ask the audience. Kneale did, and an elderly man stood up. "Mr. Kneale," said the man, "I am the only person [of the 75] in the room who has never been to school. But don't let that bother you, for I think I shall have no difficulty in getting your meaning. You just go ahead." ▲

Dredging a canal near Phoenix, Arizona, about 1920. The federal government gave control of the Salt River Project to a group of landowners who appropriated the river water for their own use.

FROM
DEPRESSION
TO
AUTONOMY

Control of scarce water continued to be an issue among Pima, Maricopa, and non-Indians after the first dams were built. In 1917 the federal government gave control of the Salt River Project (SRP) to a group of non-Indian landowners. Their control made the hard-won Maricopa legal rights to irrigation water almost meaningless.

The landowners' association attracted other potential investors because there was already income from the sale of hydroelectric power. The association sold bonds worth $8,400,000 to finance three more dams, all to be built between Salt River Reservation and Roosevelt Dam from 1925 to 1930. Mormon Flat Dam added 57,800 acre-feet of water storage capacity and 7,000 kilowatts of electrical generating capacity. (An acre-foot of water is the volume that would cover one acre of land one foot deep.) Horse Mesa Dam added 245,000 acre-feet of storage capacity and 30,000 kilowatts of generating capabil-

ity. Stewart Mountain Dam added 70,000 acre-feet to its reservoirs, and 10,000 kilowatts. These reservoirs stored floodwater as well as water diverted from the river's normal flow. As a result, no surface water flowed from the Salt River into Maricopa farmers' irrigation canals. Today, Maricopa men who grew up before 1930 recall that theirs was the last generation to know the fun of fishing in the deep pools fed by the river before it dried up.

To get water to the Maricopa, the BIA pressured the SRP into drilling a deep-tube well, to be operated by a pump. The underground well water was so salty, however, that it killed vegetable plants. Farmers had to shift to planting cotton and small grains.

Similar problems occurred on the Gila River. Coolidge Dam could not furnish the Pima with enough water to replace what was stolen from them upstream. When dam gates shut, water stopped flowing downstream alto-

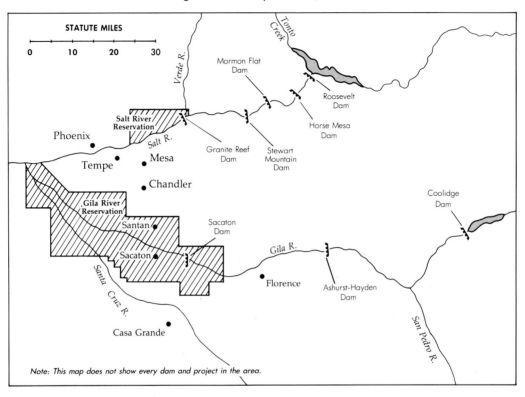

STATUTE MILES

0   10   20   30

Verde R.

Tonto Creek

Mormon Flat Dam

Roosevelt Dam

Horse Mesa Dam

Salt River Reservation

Phoenix

Salt R.

Granite Reef Dam

Stewart Mountain Dam

Mesa

Tempe

Chandler

Coolidge Dam

Gila River Reservation

Santan

Sacaton Dam

Sacaton

Gila R.

Florence

Ashurst-Hayden Dam

Santa Cruz R.

San Pedro R.

Casa Grande

Note: This map does not show every dam and project in the area.

gether, making agriculture impossible for most Pima and Maricopa. The normal fluctuations in rain and snow proved the dam's failure: For 10 years San Carlos Reservoir was never full. Not until 1941, a rare wet year, did the stream provide enough water to fill the reservoir. Despite the evidence from a decade of low runoff, BIA officials continued to believe that the high dam would work. The farmers knew otherwise.

A. H. Kneale had no previous experience in the Sonoran desert environment when he took over as BIA superintendent at Sacaton in 1930. He chose A. E. "Bert" Robinson, who did have experience, to assist him. Kneale wrote of Robinson, "He was popular with the pupils, the Indians, the employees. His farm, his garden, his dairy, hogs, poultry, apiary, surpassed any." Robinson may not have been so popular among his Indian student-helpers as Kneale believed—the helpers were not paid. This did not trouble Kneale, as the two seemed to have the same ideas about Indians.

The program they began, called *subjugation*, was meant to reorganize the farms and provide new means of irrigation. Instead, it caused the physical destruction of the age-old Pima and Maricopa fields and canals. Powerful tractors pulled trees from the earth and tugged giant earth-moving machines over the Pima's old ditches. All vegetation was removed, the land was leveled, new canals were built, and roads and fences went up. Kneale and Robinson paid no attention to soil quality. Their machines either mixed the surface humus enriched with mesquite leaves into the sterile subsoil or buried it under clay or sand.

The Pima and Maricopa could not stop Kneale and Robinson from carrying out this program, part of the San Carlos Indian Irrigation Project (SCIIP). Moreover, the BIA expected the Indian farmers to reimburse the U.S. Treasury for the subjugation costs of SCIIP and to pay for the operation and maintenance of the dams, generators, and canals.

Pima and Maricopa farmers with 10-acre irrigated allotments knew that they could not even make a living from such small tracts, much less pay the costs of subjugation or operations and maintenance. By the early 1930s, Xavier Cawker, a farmer, had emerged as leader of the Pima Business Committee. Cawker argued that when Congress passed the 1924 act that authorized Coolidge Dam, it intended that the Pima and Maricopa should receive SCIIP irrigation water free, just as the river had historically supplied it. The

BIA operated SCIIP, however, and threatened to cut off water delivery to Pima farmers if operating and maintenance fees went unpaid.

John Collier, the commissioner of Indian affairs in the Democratic reform administration of President Franklin D. Roosevelt, was far more sympathetic toward Indians than any previous holder of the office. In 1933, Collier's first year in office, he approved a three-year moratorium on the payments to SCIIP. He insisted, however, that Pima and Maricopa farmers start paying the charges again in 1936. Cawker and other community leaders knew that individual farmers could not pay the expenses. In 1936 and thereafter, the new community council stepped in and acted as a shock absorber for the farmers by paying the costs, under protest, out of its own small income.

Collier believed that the Indians should live according to their traditions, as they themselves decided and to the extent possible in modern times. He drew on his experience with the Pueblo peoples of New Mexico, whose way of life was disrupted less than most other Indians, including the poor but industrious Maricopa and Pima. Collier translated his beliefs into a radical piece of legislation, the Indian Reorganization Act (IRA). The heavily Democratic Congress passed it in 1934.

The IRA repealed the General Allotment Act of 1887, under which Indian farmers had not fared well. Repeal meant that the allotment provisions of

The BIA headquarters at Sacaton in 1919. Its well-irrigated lawn and an air-cooling system that used water falling from the towers at rear exemplify the unjust consequences of water diversion. Nearby, the Indians' crops suffered from lack of irrigation water.

the 1924 San Carlos Act were no longer in effect. As a result, the BIA could no longer allot reservation lands to individuals. Land already allotted, however, did not change status.

The IRA also authorized residents of reservations to write and approve constitutions and to set up semiautonomous governments. As self-governing communities, they would be subject to less domination by non-Indians. In 1936 residents of the Gila River Reservation voted for a constitution and bylaws, even though they already had a government that functioned according to the laws of their old Confederation. (About one-third of the tribes in the United States, including the Navajo Nation, maintained their traditional governing systems and rejected IRA-type constitutions.) The constitution divided the reservation into seven electoral districts, each of which elected members to the council. The council of the Gila River Indian Community (GRIC) then chose as governor Xavier Cawker in 1936 and 1937, and Johnson McAfee, a native of Gila Crossing and a printer and teacher, the next year.

Division into seven districts created one problem. The minority Maricopa are concentrated in District 7, which is farthest to the west. Because the Pima council majority conducted business in its own language for many years, the Yuman-speaking delegates from District 7 often did not attend meetings.

The Pima and Maricopa on Salt

A Pima home made of mesquite beams, arrowweeds, and earth, near Casa Grande in 1938. Because they could no longer grow their own food, living conditions worsened for the already-poor Pima and Maricopa during the Great Depression of the 1930s.

River Reservation also wrote their own constitution and provided for their own governance. Thus, the two groups began divergent courses of self-government despite their ethnic and historic unity. In contrast, the BIA grouped three geographically separate reserved areas into a single Papago tribe.

In the fall of 1938 the National Guard unit at Casa Grande, which included several Pima Indians, marched in the military funeral of its captain. The guard's divisional shoulder patch was a swastika, which shocked viewers who had come to loath a similar emblem used by the Nazi party of Germany. (The swastika is an ancient Indian symbol—for the Pima it represented a whirlwind—and the local guard unit

had adopted it long before Adolf Hitler's Nazi party, which meant it to symbolize European white purity.) Guard officials changed with the times by choosing a new design for their shoulder patch.

In 1940, World War II was under way in Europe. President Roosevelt thought that the United States would soon be involved, so he mobilized the National Guard. Arizona's 158th Infantry Regiment went south to protect the Panama Canal and to train for jungle warfare. After Japan attacked the U.S. naval base at Pearl Harbor, Hawaii, in December 1941, the United States entered the war in both Europe and the Far East. "The Bushmasters," as the Arizona guard unit was called, later had an outstanding record in island battles in the Pacific.

Some Pimas in the guard stood out, especially J. R. Morago, Jr. (Kisto's grandson), and Sam Thomas. Thomas had been sent from Panama to Officer Candidate School at Fort Benning, Georgia. While still a first lieutenant, he commanded his company for five months in Europe, without the pro-

motion to captain that a company commander deserved. Only after a chance meeting with General George Patton did this discrimination end: When Patton learned of the slight, he saw that Thomas got the captaincy he had earned.

There were other Pima and Maricopa war heroes. Urban Giff became the first Indian commissioned as a Marine

Left: *Ira Hayes, a 19-year-old Pima paratrooper, preparing to jump in 1943.* Right: *Two years later Hayes helped raise the U.S. flag on Iwo Jima after marines drove the Japanese off Mt. Suribachi in three days of vicious fighting. (This photograph, by Joe Rosenthal, won a Pulitzer Prize and inspired a statue that now stands outside Arlington National Cemetery.)*

Barracks housing for Japanese-Americans interned on the Gila River Reservation from 1942 to 1945 by the U.S. government. The presence of more than 13,000 additional people added to the strain on the Indians' land and water resources.

Corps officer. Pima Ira Hayes, also a marine, fought in the ferocious battle for the Pacific island of Iwo Jima, in 1945. A Pulitzer Prize–winning photograph of the victory shows six marines, Hayes among them, hoisting the U.S. flag atop the island's Mt. Suribachi.

Throughout the war, Pima and Maricopa soldiers served alongside other citizens from many ethnic groups. In the military, some Indians gave orders, and all Indians obeyed orders written and spoken in English, which they had learned along with other skills in the reservation schools. Now they established relationships with non-Indians from all over the country, shared wartime hardships with them, and became further integrated into U.S. society.

The war was also changing Indian life at home. Some federal officials feared that the large Japanese-American population in the Pacific Coast states posed a threat to national security. The Army's Western Defense Command decided to detain and intern all Japanese and Japanese-Americans, including citizens, removing them to hastily built relocation camps. The Department of War gained the cooperation of the Department of the Interior in building camps on several Indian reservations, including Gila River Reservation. By early 1943, more than 13,000 relocated Japanese-Americans were housed in ramshackle barracks at Rivers Relocation Center. Rivers rapidly became Arizona's third largest city.

Federal authorities wanted the internees to provide as much of their own food as possible by farming. They set aside some 10,000 acres of reservation land for the internees; Gila River waters went for irrigation. In late 1942 reservation governor Alexander Cannon, a farmer, had to go to Washington to protect Pima-Maricopa rights to that water.

Legal water rights were again violated in 1942 because of the war. On February 28, Secretary of War Henry Stimson signed an order allowing the Phelps Dodge Corporation, a large mining concern, to use Gila River water in its towns, mines, and smelters upstream. Until the war ended in 1945, the company diverted about 14,000 acre-feet of water annually, enough to have irrigated about 3,500 acres of Gila River Reservation land.

In 1943 the community council elected a new governor, Presbyterian missionary Alfred Jackson, a native of Santan. He served into 1944, when Gee Gage from Gila Crossing won the post. During Gage's tenure, the council made clear that it would conduct business in the Pima language as a defense against the authoritarian style of Superintendent Bert Robinson, who had replaced Kneale in 1935 and would serve for more than 20 years. In 1945, Gage resigned in order to have time for his job as a guard at the Japanese relocation center. His decision, based on economic need, reflected the Indians' gradual movement from farming to wage work.

The council replaced Gage with dairy farmer David Johnson, Sr. Twice reelected, Johnson worked to protect Pima and Maricopa rights and to cooperate with federal officials at the same time. Sometimes the two goals were not compatible. For instance, on the last day of 1945 attorneys for Phelps Dodge made the BIA a take-it-or-leave-it offer of $275,000 for water that the mining company had taken from the Gila River during the war. Interior Department officials accepted the offer; Governor Johnson persuaded a hurriedly convened council to approve it in special session. What could have been a small financial windfall for the tribal community, however, quickly became smaller. A few months after the payment was made, federal officials turned over half of it to the San Carlos Irrigation Drainage District—a non-Indian organization.

The end of the war would bring more changes and improvements to Pima and Maricopa life. In 1948 the Arizona Supreme Court reversed one of the state's most unjust laws against Indians. In a decision 20 years earlier, the court had held, in *Porter v. Hall*, that Indians living on reserved areas could not vote for state or federal officials. This case followed a congressional act decreeing that Indians could vote if their state of residence allowed. Arizona, like most states, was slow to grant its resident Indians this basic right of citizenship. Then in 1948—following the outstanding display of bravery in the war by such men as Ira Hayes, Sam Thomas, and J. R. Morago, Jr., as well as Indians from around the country—

the state court ruled, in *Harrison v. Laveen*, that Indians could vote.

Prewar legal discrimination continued to affect the Pima and Maricopa. In a crucial 1935 case a federal judge had approved the Gila River Decree, apportioning irrigation water taken from the stream. The reservation business committee had hired an attorney, but the judge refused to let him speak, holding that only government lawyers could represent Indians. This was, of course, a contradiction: How could a government lawyer represent Indians in challenging a government action or ruling? Not surprisingly, Pima and Maricopa water rights were not adequately protected by the 1935 decree.

Then in 1949, for the first time, GRIC obtained government approval to hire its own attorney. It hired Z. Simpson Cox as the first general counsel; he had come to their notice for his brave defense of Japanese-Americans during the war. Cox began by insisting that Pima members of the council stop debating in their own language, which neither he nor the Maricopa delegates from District 7 could understand. Cox was pushing for integration within the community. He also strove to integrate the Pima and Maricopa into national life.

In 1951, Cox filed suit before the Indian Claims Commission, which had been established by Congress to hear unsettled Indian claims against the United States. Yet, when the commission dissolved in 1978, it had not decided most GRIC claims, especially those involving crucial water rights.

J. R. Morago, Jr., a Pima, was a World War II hero and, later, accountant for the reservation farm. As governor of Gila River Reservation from 1954 to 1960, he helped revise the community's 1936 constitution.

Through the late 1930s and the World War II years, Superintendent Robinson had overseen extensive farming on reserved lands that had never been allotted to individuals. This land base was greatly increased when the Rivers Relocation Center closed and its large farm was returned to the reservation. War veterans wanted the GRIC to gradually enter the farming business in order to generate income.

Alfred Jackson, elected governor again in 1951, approached Robinson with a request for the council to start managing a few hundred acres. Robinson, evidently expecting that Indian managers would fail, turned the entire farming enterprise over to the council. Sam Thomas became the farm manager and J. R. Morago the farm accountant. In spite of their lack of experience in managing such a large enterprise, Thomas and Morago soon made the big farm profitable. It became the largest single employer on the reservation, with 100 to 300 workers, depending on the season. This achievement is important, because it represents the success of Thomas and Morago as well as most Pima and Maricopa veterans in the postwar period. Ira Hayes, on the other hand, did not adjust as well. He died on the reservation, a victim of alcoholism, only 10 years after he had come to national attention at Iwo Jima.

In 1952 and again the next year the council chose as governor Loyde A. Allison, a tall, powerful farmer who looked as though he might have led war parties if he had lived a century earlier. Allison sought to reduce strife between his people and their neighbors. His approach is illustrated by his treatment of the El Paso Natural Gas Company, which had laid a natural-gas pipeline across the Gila River Reservation. Governor Allison invited the company's board of directors to dine across the border in Ciudad Juarez, Mexico, as guests of the Pima community. That social exchange strengthened Allison's belief in the essential goodness of people, for it ended years of bickering between the council and the company. Frequent and close cooperation between the two sides grew. Company officials helped community employees find scarce machine parts and even established a scholarship program for students.

In 1954 the council elected J. R. Morago, Jr., as governor and reelected him annually through 1960. Morago and Cox worked together on a drive to amend the 1936 constitution to give the council more power and to avoid annual replacement of the governor. Voters approved the new constitution, which provides that the governor and lieutenant governor be directly elected for three-year terms. Nelson Jose won the first direct election and served as governor from 1962 to 1965.

The next few years were marked for all Americans by demands for civil rights for all minorities and by the social programs of President Lyndon B. Johnson that he called the Great Society. Loyde Allison, elected governor twice more for the years 1965–71, capitalized on the many opportunities these new federal programs offered. To improve life on the Gila River Reservation, Allison supervised the creation of a development plan called "It Must Happen." The plan guided community policies for many years, even after Allison's terms as governor had ended.

The first problem the plan's developers decided to address was the lack of jobs. Allison and others recognized that the Gila River Decree limited the extent of farming on the reservation. Pima and Maricopa needed more non-farm jobs in order to earn cash income. Some already commuted from Districts 6 and 7 to jobs in Phoenix. The It Must Happen plan called for an industrial park to be built nearby so that Indians could work closer to home.

The plan bore fruit in the form of the Pima-Chandler Industrial Park, located near Interstate Highway 10 (I-10) at the point where the road crosses the reservation's northern boundary. By 1977, 16 firms had taken leases there for various light industries. The firms employed 700 people, one-third of them Indians. In 1967 the community developed Firebird Lake and a $2,000,000 marina across the road, using pumped water that was too salty for plants. At an I-10 interchange farther south, the community erected its architecturally dramatic Arts and Crafts Center.

The federal Community Action Project provided funding to construct a large, single-story building in each of Gila River's seven districts. These seven centers now house various activities, perhaps the most important of which are Head Start classes for preschool-age children. Head Start has been very important for the Maricopa and Pima (as it is for other minority groups). It prepares children from Piman- or Yuman-speaking families to enter school by teaching them English and study skills.

The district centers include kitchens, so the community initiated a pro-

Some of the first Pima and Maricopa children to enroll in the Head Start program on Salt River Reservation, mid-1960s. Head Start helps children from low-income homes learn English and study skills before starting school.

A Maricopa woman on the Gila River Reservation applies earth for insulation to a new house. Though the house's design is modern, some of its materials are traditional.

gram to provide hot, nutritious lunches for elderly people. The centers also serve as meeting halls for the community council and as the place where district officials report regularly to the people who elect them. Numerous community activities make these buildings true social centers where people gain a stronger sense of district unity.

The council headquarters was also built with the help of federal funding. The 17 council members sit in comfortable chairs behind a semicircular wooden desk in the meeting chamber, like members of any large city council.

The headquarters has offices for the governor, lieutenant governor, secretary, planning and evaluation staff, enrollment office, attorney, and others. Other departments spill over into older structures inherited from the federal government.

A pronounced change in federal activities on Indian reservations began in 1969, when President Richard M. Nixon altered the historic relationship between the BIA and Indian peoples. Nixon ordered the bureau to contract with reservation governments to furnish many local services, instead of relying on non-Indian federal employees. This change provided more jobs for Indians near their homes and extended their involvement in and control over local affairs.

The Pima leader to face the next decade of change was Alexander Lewis, who had served as Allison's lieutenant governor before being elected governor in 1971. Reelected three times, Lewis served a total of 12 years, longer than any other governor. During his term, the Nixon administration tried to end the Johnson-era War on Poverty, although Congress continued many of the programs that were beneficial to Indians. For most of his tenure, Lewis was able to keep relatively large sums of federal money flowing to Gila River Reservation, despite the shifts brought on by Nixon's policies.

Following the It Must Happen plan, Lewis and the GRIC obtained the first federal Model Cities grant made to any

Indian reservation. This program of the Department of Housing and Urban Development (HUD) started a new era in Pima and Maricopa living, with mixed results.

In the 1880s the BIA had begun a program of giving Pima and Maricopa a free wagon if they built an adobe house. The traditional pole-and-thatch houses, typically insulated by a layer of earth on top, were gradually replaced. Federal funds helped General Antonio Azul build a two-story adobe house, the largest on Gila River Reservation. The new, Mexican-style home had insulation advantages, and most families eventually built adobe houses. Yet adobe did not entirely suit the needs of the Pima. They modified the new design by alternating layers of sunbaked-earth bricks with wooden blocks to create a "sandwich" house. Its thick walls are sturdy and insulate well against Sonoran desert heat; yet they cost little to construct.

HUD, conversely, insisted on standardized housing for the entire community, to be constructed of "standard" manufactured materials that tended to be expensive. To save money on plumbing, the Indian Division of the U.S. Public Health Service (which installs pipes for water and disposal systems) prefers that house sites be close together. The BIA, which builds the streets and sidewalks, agrees. HUD housing is easily recognizable: The walls are earth-colored concrete blocks, the roofs are low-pitched, and the va-riety of floor plans is limited. The houses are arranged in clusters, but few Pima who live in HUD housing like living so close to one another. Before the 1970s, Pima families lived at a distance from each other. Maricopa families still live in scattered housing because their homes are on their allotted irrigated farms, not in HUD subdivisions. Overall, the new housing on the reservation makes it look something like the poorest suburban developments in the surrounding area.

Integration comes slowly, as does restitution. In 1978 the U.S. Court of Claims decided an important part of the community's suit concerning the San Carlos project, which had originally been brought before the Indian Claims Commission. The court held that in the 1924 San Carlos Act, Congress had not intended the Pima and Maricopa to pay the cost of operating and maintaining the irrigation project. Furthermore, the ruling called for the United States to pay back, with interest, all of the project's operating and maintenance fees collected from the community after 1936.

This financial gain, however, did not bring the improvements it might have. Prohibited from charging those fees, the BIA neglected to maintain the equipment and machinery. Coolidge Dam's electrical generators ground to a halt in 1983. Ashurst-Hayden diversion dam, on the other hand, still works. It sends water into canals that serve not only Indians but also non-Indian farmers and city dwellers. ▲

The courtyard of the Gila River Arts and Crafts Center. The center, built in the 1970s, also contains a museum and a restaurant. The doorway in the base of the tower echos the shape of the doorway of a traditional Pima house.

LEARNING
TO
SUCCEED

The southwestern United States in the latter half of the 20th century continues to experience a population boom that places an enormous strain on the region's water resources. Migrants from colder areas are drawn as if by a magnet to the usually snow-free winters of the Sonoran desert. In 1935, when the Gila River Decree was signed, only about 460,000 people lived in Arizona. By 1960 there were 1,300,000 residents, and by 1985 nearly 3,200,000 people lived there.

Most of these migrants move to cities near the Gila River and its tributaries. Half of Arizona's inhabitants, in fact, live in a dozen cities in the Salt River valley. The urban sprawl stretches from the western edge of Salt River Reservation to the northern edge of Gila River Reservation. A community of older people nestles along a section of Gila River Reservation's northern boundary. Farther west, the paved streets of greater Phoenix extend south into Districts 6 and 7 of the reservation.

Another 15 percent of Arizona's population lives in 6 cities along the Santa Cruz River. That river once flowed into the Gila a few miles above the Salt; now it is dry. City residents and pecan and cotton farmers use all of its surface and underground water.

Every year, more farmland in southern Arizona is paved over for shopping malls and suburban streets. This shift affects both water use and price. Homeowners who water their lawns and plants consume only about one-third as much water per acre as farmers, who must irrigate crops. Because of the high cost of water-delivery and sewage-disposal systems, cities must charge their customers more than farmers can afford to pay for a given amount of water. As the population increases, the cost of providing water also rises. Pima-Maricopa water rights therefore become increasingly significant.

The Pima and Maricopa have adjusted to their changing social environment in many ways. On the legal front, Z. Simpson Cox and his sons Alfred and Alan continue to represent the Gila River Indian Community (GRIC) in water-rights cases. In 1969 the federal district court in Tucson ordered the Gila River water commissioner to reduce the amount of water that canal companies in Safford Valley were diverting "in disregard" of the time-immemorial rights of the Maricopa and Pima. This was only the second change made to the terms of the decree since 1935.

In 1977, Cox prevailed in getting a mining firm to pay damages and future fees for water it diverted from Mineral Creek, a small tributary of the Gila. With that case settled, in 1979 he brought suit for the community in federal court against water users on the San Pedro River, another tributary of the Gila. The court has yet to make a general determination of the community's rights to the waters of tributaries because the 1935 decree applies only to the main stream.

Water scarcity across Arizona makes water rights a key issue. The courts are to rule separately on cases involving each of the major river basins. For example, one judge is assigned to the Gila–Salt River watershed case. In late 1987 this judge heard expert testimony from hydrologists for the GRIC, the U.S. Department of Justice, several Arizona cities, and major business corporations. The case may take 20 years or more to complete.

In the meantime, individual Pima and Maricopa must face more immediate difficulties as they battle to succeed in fast-changing Arizona. Few young people today want to farm. Both water and irrigable fields are scarce on their reservations, because of the old

Rodney Lewis, son of a Pima father and a Mojave mother, is an attorney who represents the Gila River Indian Community. A better-educated generation is providing new leadership.

federal allotment policy. Few allottees are still alive, and their heirs, after three or more generations, typically own only a fraction of the original 10 acres. Would-be farmers have to lease tiny parcels from many owners to put together a farm of contiguous plots of land. Identifying, contacting, and persuading heirs to lease their land is so time consuming and expensive that only extremely dedicated farmers keep at it.

Some workers commute from Blackwater Village, at the eastern end of the reservation, to downtown Phoenix, a round-trip of more than 100 miles. So many villages are home to city workers that they have become primarily bedroom suburbs. The reverse commute, from city to suburb, is also common now. Rodney Lewis, for example, lives in affluent Scottsdale and commutes to Sacaton. He studied law at the University of California, Los Angeles, and became the first Arizona Indian to pass the state bar examination. He practiced law with the Cox family firm until the GRIC made him its general counsel. One well-paid Pima secretary also became a reverse commuter after learning the cost of renting a HUD-financed apartment near Sacaton from the community's housing authority. She decided to rent an apartment in the city instead and travel daily to her job in Sacaton.

As much as they may want to remain on their ancient lands, the Pima and Maricopa, like everyone else, must go where the jobs are. The 1980 census counted 10,771 Indians in Phoenix, constituting 1.4 percent of the city's population. (In 1987 about the same number of persons—10,688—lived on the Gila River Reservation.) Members of tribes from all over the country have migrated to Phoenix, but Pimas are the most numerous there.

Federal funding diminished for programs to benefit minorities and the poor during President Ronald Reagan's administration. The decrease in funds that handicapped former governor Lewis during his last term has burdened his successors. Dana R. Norris,

Sr., elected governor in 1982, sought alternative sources of income for the community. He welcomed a proposal by Florida investors to build a jai alai fronton, or arena, next to Pima-Chandler Industrial Park. (Jai alai is a handball-like game of Basque origin in which players use baskets strapped to their wrists to hurl a ball against a backboard.) Florida, with a much larger population than Arizona, has several popular frontons where betting is the main attraction. Gambling on human sports (in contrast to dogs or horses) is illegal in Arizona, however, so the state attorney general blocked the project.

Having served as lieutenant governor under Lewis, Donald Antone defeated Norris in a highly charged 1984 election. Antone presided over a council that faced more complicated issues. For example, in 1985 hundreds of Pima and Maricopa met in all 7 districts to furnish information and policy guidelines for a master water-use plan to update the It Must Happen plan of 20 years before. In another instance, Santan Industrial Park, on the reservation, ran into trouble with a tenant who was manufacturing explosives without adequate safeguards; an explosion there killed two employees. The GRIC farm enterprise, managed by a non-Indian after Sam Thomas retired, lost money year after year.

Other contentious issues have arisen. The claims court decided in three decisions from 1983 to 1985 that the government owed damages to the community for lands lost outside the reserved areas. A woman who has run unsuccessfully for governor then led a drive demanding that the GRIC distribute most of the award money to individuals. The chance for a cash award impelled many Pima and Maricopa to officially enroll in the community for the first time. This interest in money brought the enrolled population up to more than 12,000.

Many Indian children now in school can expect eventually to outdo their elders. After completing elementary school on Gila River Reservation, students board buses to high schools in cities around the reservation—Casa Grande to the south, Coolidge to the east, Chandler or Phoenix's South Mountain to the north. Some parents, concerned about the long bus rides or other dangers, drive their children to and from school. Among the outstanding recent students are a boy who has received a congressional medal awarded to high-school scholars and a young woman gymnast who has traveled to the Soviet Union for an international competition. Others, too, are excellent students and take part in extracurricular activities despite the time they must spend commuting. The son of one GRIC official played football at Casa Grande High School and was also a member of the marching band; he then enrolled at the University of Arizona.

Most young Pima and Maricopa learn business skills and English in school so they can find a job in the city. John Lewis, Rodney's younger brother, is typical of those who have achieved off-reservation success through education. Lewis, the son of a Pima Presbyterian minister and a Mojave mother, earned a bachelor's degree at the University of Oklahoma and a master's degree at the University of Arizona, both in anthropology. He is now executive director of the Arizona Intertribal Council.

Not all Pima and Maricopa students are so successful. Many, like Indians elsewhere in North America, have difficulty overcoming the poverty into which they are born. Poverty can lead to crime, and Gila River Reservation has a jail and a juvenile detention center. Alcoholism is probably the most serious problem, and sometimes a deadly one, afflicting about one-third of the residents. Alcohol consumption causes some persons to become violent, and it is particularly dangerous to those suffering from diabetes. The Pima, according to the National Institutes for Health, have the nation's highest-known diabetes rate—half of all persons over age 35 contract diabetes, compared to about 6 percent nationally.

Diabetes and its side effects become more serious as people age. It causes circulatory problems that sometimes result in gangrene, which can be treated only by surgical amputation of the affected limb. It can also lead to blindness, stroke, and kidney failure and has left more than a few elderly patients confined to wheelchairs. Sometimes diabetes is related to obesity, which is very common among the Pima, to some extent a result of inadequate nutrition. Many of the poorer individuals subsist on a diet of potatoes, bread, and other starchy foods. Their traditional diet is now beyond their reach, for they cannot catch fish in a dry riverbed and they cannot afford to buy much meat or many fresh fruits and vegetables. Diabetes, alcoholism, and other illnesses keep female life expectancy down to 64 years compared to the national average of 79 years; for Pima men the figure is 51 years, compared to 70 nationally.

Still, there are reasons for optimism. In the 1987 election, Lieutenant Governor Thomas White defeated former governor Antone. The new lieutenant governor, William R. Rhodes, had been a Maricopa County sheriff and then chief judge of the reservation court for 12 years, giving him special insight into the community's workings. Aside from being a distinguished public servant, Rhodes is also probably the reservation's most successful entrepreneur. He set up a tobacco shop at an I-10 interchange, attracting customers with low prices. (States cannot tax tobacco products—or anything else—sold on reservations.)

Another success story is that of the two young Maricopa women who run a cattle ranch (inherited from their grandfather) on arid lands in the western end of the reservation. Their complaints about restrictive rules and regulations are much like those of conservative Texas ranchers who criticize Congress. Their occupation forces them to gamble on the beef market like any

Two Pima boys prepare to dye Easter eggs. Since most Pima and Maricopa became Presbyterian or Roman Catholic in the late 1800s, the celebration of Christian holidays has largely replaced observances of their traditional religion.

other rancher in the United States, yet they enjoy every day they spend in the saddle on their favorite horses, surveying the expanse of their people's ancient lands. They are living examples of how the Pima and Maricopa can once again live with dignity.

Today's young Pima have an identity problem stemming from the many distinctions between them and their non-Indian neighbors. Few of them or their ancestors have married non-Indians, so the Pima continue to look like New World natives. They are also culturally different from any of the several groups of newcomers, and growing up on Gila River Reservation accentuates their awareness that they exist outside U.S. society. Furthermore, the ongoing legal battle—since 1857—for their time-immemorial water rights acts to drive a wedge between the Pima and their neighbors. Attorneys for the Indians have at times been successful in this battle, and in general the courts have agreed with their position, but federal efforts to protect the water rights have often been lax. The resulting sense that non-Indians do not care about Indians' rights also alienates the Pima from the larger society.

When Pima became Presbyterians and Roman Catholics, they wholeheartedly committed themselves and their descendants to living as much as possible like the Christian newcomers to the Sonoran desert. There are, however, limits to the advantages of their conversion. The Judeo-Christian tradition offers no stories of the origin of Piman-speaking people or of other New World natives. Even their religion reminds Pima and Maricopa students that they differ from newcomers.

Since Pima became Christians, no native religious leader has conducted the traditional rituals. Nor does anyone regularly retell the ancient legends about how the River People came to live in the Gila River valley. Pima students,

Pima teenagers with some materials for making traditional baskets—willow reeds, seedpods of the devil's-claw plant (right), and a water jar for soaking the pods. Many Pima teenagers today are learning their own culture and heritage.

almost all of whom speak the Pima language, have to search hard to find copies of Pima legends, even in abridged English translations. Conversely, newspaper and magazine articles about the many ruined native settlements in the valley, though often oversimplified, are widely available. Pima *are* reminded that they and their forebears have very rapidly altered their culture to cope with changing circumstances.

In one sense, Maricopa students face a lesser identity problem than Pima students do. The migration eastward by the Maricopa from the Colorado River occurred recently enough that storytellers still recount it today. In sharp contrast, there is no traditional explanation of when the Pima first reached the middle Gila River valley. Their oral history records no migration, leading many to believe that Pima have lived on the Gila River longer than oral history can pinpoint. On the other hand, histories written by non-Indians that place the River People near the Gila reach back only to 1694. Archaeological research suggests, but has yet to show conclusively, that Pima ancestors, thought by some to be the Hohokam, were living in the middle Gila River valley and irrigating with canals for a thousand or more years before Europeans arrived in the Southwest.

Whatever the prehistoric links, there has been one constant for the Pima and Maricopa since the 17th century: the struggle to find enough water

A Maricopa woman shows her granddaughter how to make pottery. Although young people increasingly participate in non-Indian society, older people still carry on and teach many tribal practices.

in the Sonoran desert to sustain life. The Pima and Maricopa have suffered through their worst years at the hands of ruthless investors and land grabbers, and the fight to undo the damage will never end. Descendants of the region's original inhabitants are, however, gaining skills in law, business, farming, and community organization that they are utilizing to win back the water and lands that were once theirs. They cannot return to their traditional way of life, but the Pima and Maricopa can integrate their new skills with their traditions. They can succeed in wresting a livelihood from a social and economic environment that is every bit as harsh as the desert itself. ▲

BIBLIOGRAPHY

Dale, Edward Everett. *The Indians of the Southwest.* Norman: University of Oklahoma Press, 1974.

Dobyns, Henry F. "The Kohatk: Oasis and Ak Chin Horticulturalists." *Ethnohistory* 21 (Fall 1974): 317–28.

———. *From Fire to Flood: Historic Human Destruction of Sonoran Desert Riverine Oases.* Socorro, CA: Ballena Press, 1981.

Dobyns, Henry F., Paul H. Ezell, and Greta S. Ezell. "Death of a Society: The Halchidhoma." *Ethnohistory* 10 (Spring 1963): 105–61.

Ezell, Paul H. *The Hispanic Acculturation of the Gila River Pimas.* Menasha, WI: American Anthropological Association Memoir 90, 1961.

———. *The Maricopas: An Identification from Documentary Sources.* Tucson: University of Arizona Anthropological Papers No. 6, 1961.

Russell, Frank. *The Pima Indians.* Tucson: University of Arizona Press, 1975.

Shaw, Anna Moore. *A Pima Past.* Tucson: University of Arizona Press, 1974.

Spier, Leslie. *Yuman Tribes of the Gila River.* New York: Cooper Square, 1970.

Stratton, R. B. *Captivity of the Oatman Girls.* Lincoln: University of Nebraska Press, 1983.

Sturtevant, William H., and Alfonso Ortiz, eds. *Handbook of North American Indians.* Vol. 10, *Southwest,* 149–60. Washington, D.C.: Smithsonian Institution, 1983.

Webb, George. *A Pima Remembers.* Tucson: University of Arizona Press, 1969.

THE PIMA-MARICOPA AT A GLANCE

TRIBES *Pima and Maricopa*

CULTURE AREA *Southwest*

GEOGRAPHY *Gila and Salt River oases in the southern Arizona region of the Sonoran desert*

LINGUISTIC FAMILIES *Piman and Yuman*

CURRENT POPULATION *approximately 12,000*

FIRST CONTACT *Brigadier General Stephen W. Kearny, U.S. Army, 1846*

FEDERAL STATUS *recognized. Many Pima and Maricopa live on two reservations, Gila and Salt River; most others live in Phoenix, Arizona, and nearby cities.*

adobe A building material or brick made of sun-dried earth and straw.

agent A person appointed by the Bureau of Indian Affairs to supervise U.S. government programs on a reservation and/or in a specific region. After 1908 the title "superintendent" replaced "agent."

allotment U.S. policy, first applied in 1887, to break up tribally owned reservations by assigning individual farms and ranches to Indians. Intended as much to discourage traditional communal activities as to encourage private farming and assimilate Indians into mainstream American life.

Apache Traditionally nomadic Indian people who live in the southwestern United States and Mexico and belong to the Athapaskan language family.

Army Corps of Engineers A department of the U.S. armed forces, started by the Continental Congress in 1775 to open up and maintain navigation routes on the Ohio and Mississippi rivers. Today it is in charge of any governmental survey and development plans for federally owned lands.

Bureau of Indian Affairs (BIA) A U.S. government agency created within the Department of the Interior in 1849. Originally intended to manage trade and other relations with Indians, the BIA now seeks, through the programs it develops and implements, to encourage Indians to manage their own affairs and to improve their educational opportunities and general social and economic well-being.

environment The natural and cultural space that a society occupies; includes climate, geographical features, and plant and animal life.

fermentation The process by which the pulp and/or juice of vegetables or fruits is made into alcohol.

Forty-niner A person who traveled to California in search of gold in 1849.

Gadsden Purchase The 1853 treaty by which Mexico ceded to the United States what is now the southernmost portion of Arizona and the southwestern tip of New Mexico. The U.S. government wanted to build a railroad across the region, which included the Pima and Maricopa homelands.

harrow A wood or metal framework set with teeth or spikes, which is dragged across plowed soil to break up clods.

Indian Claims Commission (ICC) A U.S. government body created by an act of Congress in 1946 to hear and rule on claims brought by Indians against the United States. These claims stem from unfulfilled treaty terms, such as nonpayment for land sold by the Indians.

Indian Reorganization Act (IRA) The 1934 federal law that ended the policy of allotting plots of land to individuals and encouraged the political and economic development of reservation communities. The act provided for the creation of autonomous tribal governments.

irrigation The routing of water to cultivated fields through ditches and canals.

jai alai An indoor ball game. Players use hand-held baskets to hurl a ball with great speed.

land subjugation The process of clearing plants and trees from a tract of land, grading or leveling its surface, digging irrigation and drainage ditches, and generally preparing the land for cultivation.

mesquite A spiny species of tree or shrub that forms extensive thickets in the southwestern United States and northwestern Mexico. The tree produces edible pods that are nutritious and rich in sugar.

Mormons Members of the Church of Jesus Christ of Latter Day Saints founded by Joseph Smith in the 1820s in the northeastern United States. Mormons began migrating to Utah in 1847. Some settled in Pima-Maricopa territory in the 1870s.

navait An intoxicating beverage made by fermenting the fruit of the saguaro cactus; drunk by the Pimas during the rain ceremony.

Navajo Traditionally pastoral Indian people in the Southwest; the most populous Indian group in the United States. The Navajo speak a southern Athapaskan language closely related to that of the Apache.

Pima-Maricopa Confederation An agreement, made in 1750, between the Pima and Maricopa tribes that combined the fighting strength of the two tribes, making them better able to contend with the invading Apache. The Confederation, which functioned through the 19th century, provided important assistance to U.S. military forces in the area.

prehistory Anything that happened before written records existed for a given locality. In North America, anything earlier than the first contact with Europeans is considered to be prehistoric.

public domain In U.S. history, unowned land that was bought or won through treaties with foreign powers, or land seized from an Indian group by the federal government. Most public domain land was eventually sold or given away to U.S. citizens.

Quechan A Yuman-speaking tribe living in several villages near the junction of the Gila and Colorado rivers.

record rod A type of time marker made by carving symbols on a long, thin, wooden rod. These symbols indicated important events rather than divisions of time and were used as memory aids by storytellers as they related past events.

redoubt An enclosed defensive fortification. The redoubts built by Pima ancestors served as warehouses, dwellings, and ceremonial halls at various times in tribal history.

reservation, reserve A tract of land set aside by treaty for Indian occupation and use.

saguaro cactus A giant tube-shaped, ribbed cactus found in the deserts of the western United States. The plant provided the fruit that Pimas used to make the intoxicant *navait*.

territory The governmental status of a defined region of the U.S. that is not a state but may achieve statehood. The states of Arizona, Arkansas, and Oklahoma, among others, were once territories or parts of a territory.

tribe A society consisting of several or many separate communities united by kinship, culture, and language, and such other social factors as clans, religious organizations, and economic and political institutions.

trust The relationship between the federal government and many Indian tribes, dating from the late 19th century. Government agents managed Indians' business dealings, including land transactions and rights to national resources, because the Indians were alleged to be legally incompetent to manage their own affairs.

vahki A Pima house of worship and community meetinghouse, where the New Year festival was held.

PICTURE CREDITS

HENRY F. DOBYNS received a B.A. and M.A. in anthropology from the University of Arizona and a Ph.D. in anthropology from Cornell University. He has taught at Cornell, Prescott College, and the Universities of Kentucky, Florida, and Wisconsin-Parkside. His ethnohistorical research and investigations have taken him through much of western South America and northern Mexico, and, in the United States, among Indian groups, Hispanic mountain villagers, and rural Kentuckians. He is the author or coauthor of 35 books, including volumes on the Apache, Papago, Havasupai, Navajo, and Hopi Indians, and of numerous articles and reviews.

FRANK W. PORTER III, general editor of INDIANS OF NORTH AMERICA, is director of the Chelsea House Foundation for American Indian Studies. He holds a B.A., M.A., and Ph.D. from the University of Maryland. He has done extensive research concerning the Indians of Maryland and Delaware and is the author of numerous articles on their history, archaeology, geography, and ethnography. He was formerly director of the Maryland Commission on Indian Affairs and American Indian Research and Resource Institute, Gettysburg, Pennsylvania, and he has received grants from the Delaware Humanities Forum, the Maryland Committee for the Humanities, the Ford Foundation, and the National Endowment for the Humanities, among others. Dr. Porter is the author of *The Bureau of Indian Affairs* in the Chelsea House KNOW YOUR GOVERNMENT series.